MARKETING
like
JESUS

25 Strategies to Change the World

DARREN SHEARER

HIGH BRIDGE BOOKS
HOUSTON

Marketing Like Jesus: 25 Strategies to Change the World
by Darren Shearer

Printed in the United States of America
ISBN (Paperback): 978-1-940024-13-4
ISBN (eBook): 978-1-940024-26-4

Unless otherwise indicated, Bible quotations are taken from *The New American Standard Version — Updated Edition*. NASB. Copyright © 2000 by Zondervan.

Scripture quotations marked NLT are taken from the Holy Bible, New Living Translation, copyright © 1996, 2004, 2015 by Tyndale House Foundation. Used by permission of Tyndale House Publishers, Inc., Carol Stream, Illinois 60188. All rights reserved.

www.TheologyofBusiness.com

For Marie …
my beautiful, virtuous, and world-changing wife

CONTENTS

PREFACE

While most books written about Jesus Christ focus primarily on *what* and *why* he was marketing his message, the aim of *Marketing Like Jesus* is to explore *how* he marketed.

Before you read this book, please note that this is not intended to be a religious book. This is a marketing book to help you understand how to model your marketing strategies after the most influential man in history. This book will help you with your marketing efforts, regardless of your religious affiliation.

Each of the 25 *Marketing Like Jesus* strategies shared in this book has been categorized into one of five main, essential functions of marketers: 1) Serve, 2) Target, 3) Connect, 4) Lead, and 5) Multiply.

When explaining each of the 25 *Marketing Like Jesus* strategies in this book, I used the following general framework with the goal of helping you, the reader, to understand and apply each strategy:

1. Introduction of the marketing strategy
2. Example(s) of how Jesus applied the strategy
3. Example(s) of how the strategy has been applied by marketers in recent history

My vision is to see that every leader and aspiring leader seeking to make a positive impact on the world would apply each of the *Marketing Like Jesus* strategies to change the world around them. My aim is to convince you that, when it comes to spreading messages that are good for humanity, there is no greater role model for us to follow than Jesus.

In recent days, I have seen the application of these strategies enhance the impact of entrepreneurs, missionaries, public servants, direct-sales professionals, teachers, authors, pastors, business executives, nonprofit leaders, and others. I am certain that these marketing strategies will help you and your organization to go to the next level of positive impact on the world.

JESUS, THE MARKETER

magine sitting in a "Marketing 101" class in college. Your professor says,

> Class, today, we have a special guest professor who will lead today's class. This man is the single greatest marketing genius of all time. Based on the astonishing number of people around the world who claim to be his followers, no person in the history of the world has made a more profound impact on the hearts and minds of people and cultures than this man.
>
> While about 60,000 people would have witnessed some part of his ministry in Israel some 2,000 years ago,[1] approximately one out of every three people in the world today claims to be his follower.[2]
>
> Besides the religion he inspired, Christianity, all other major world religions are still concentrated around the areas where they were founded. As noted by Andrew Walls, Christianity is the exception.[3] A hundred years ago, 80 percent of Jesus' followers lived in Europe and the United States. Today, about 70 percent of his

followers live in the Southern Hemisphere, South America, Africa, and the East.[4] Christianity has been on the move since it began. By 2050, only one-fifth of the world's Christians will be non-Hispanic whites. Most of these will be conservative and charismatic.[5]

The calendar system used by most of the world is based upon his birthday.

Most commercial retailers in the United States can stay in business from year to year only because of the gift sales generated in conjunction with Christmas, the world-wide celebration of his birthday.

The *Bible*, which tells his story, continues to be the best-selling book in history. Despite ongoing attempts to burn it, ban it, and ridicule it throughout history, an estimated six billion copies have been printed. Translations have been made available in more than 2,000 languages and dialects. It continues to be the best-selling book, year after year, but the *New York Times Best-Seller List* and others started excluding it many years ago due to its consistent dominance on the list.[6]

Ninety-two percent of the first 138 colleges and universities founded in America were begun specifically for his followers, including Harvard and Yale.

According to Harvard professor Harvey Cox, the words of this man's famous Sermon on the Mount are "the most luminous, most quoted, most analyzed, most contested, most influential moral and religious discourse in all of human history."[7]

The movie made about his life, *The Jesus Film*, remains the most-watched movie of all time.[8]

For many centuries, people all over the world have named their children after his followers.

Throughout history and even today, people have attempted to snuff out his message through persecuting his followers with mockery, social isolation, imprisonment, and even execution. Yet, his followers continue to multiply exponentially throughout the world.

Please welcome to today's Marketing 101 class ... Jesus Christ.

Does this seem bizarre to you? Is it odd, to say the least, to think of Jesus as a marketing expert and practitioner?

MARKETER: "ONE WHO SEEKS A RESPONSE"

Before we move forward, let's clarify some working definitions:

Marketer – "one who seeks a specific response"
Marketing – "the art & science of strategic influence"

Whether we're trying to strategically influence constituents, customers, members, employees, donors, friends, or even our family members, we are all trying to influence people to respond in specific ways. That is why you picked up this book in the first place; you're a marketer. A strategic influencer. An intentional leader. More than that, you want to be a good one.

We, marketers, are vital to the public, private, and social sectors of society. Without marketers, nothing gets done because nobody gets involved. Marketers express the messages and purposes of a society.

The problem is that not all marketers have a noble purpose. That is why we have good marketers and bad marketers. Simply put, good marketers influence like Jesus Christ; bad marketers do not.

Marketing is often the term missing from most of today's teaching on leadership, which is usually presented through the lens of a large organization (i.e., lots of employees). In such leadership models, one is only considered to be a "leader" if he or she *has people under* him or her who report to him or her. So, the focus of such leadership teaching emphasizes topics such as "how to present a performance report," "how to lead a staff meeting," "how to properly hire and fire employees," etc. Yes, these roles of the leader are important, but they have dominated the conversation about leadership.

First and foremost, leaders are marketers. John Quincy Adams said, "If your actions inspire others to dream more, learn more, do more, and become more, you are a leader." Inspiring others to change is what marketing is all about. Marketers are intentional leaders and strategic influencers who motivate people to take action. They understand that a great message won't do anybody any good if nobody hears it. They put arms and legs on their leadership. They do not just share a message; they pursue a response that is mutually beneficial for both the influencer and the one being influenced.

At any level of an organization, marketers apply a vision to and through an organization. Where there is a lack of strategic influencers, there is a lack of purpose. Where there is no purpose, there is nothing to market. It is about deliberate leadership, influence with an engine and a steering wheel. Whether we're talking about a business, church, non-profit, educational institution, or governmental organization, marketing is the means through which an organization expresses its purpose. It isn't simply a function of an organization; marketing is why organizations form and exist in the first place. Purpose. Message. Service to humanity. Marketers embody this expression of their organizations.

Are you a marketer? I am not just asking if you supply a message, cause, product, or service for people. Like Jesus, do you deliberately and strategically pursue specific responses and reactions from people? Remember, a marketer is "one who seeks a response." What responses are you seeking from people?

JESUS INFLUENCED PEOPLE STRATEGICALLY

Most of us have accepted the concept of Jesus as a carpenter, leader, and a religious figure. Many of us even consider him to be our savior, healer, friend, master, and God. Much has been written about the theological, historical, and even sociological implications of Jesus' life, death, resurrection, and ministry. In fact, there are more biographies about Jesus than there are about any other human—more than

100,000 biographies about him in English alone![9] In the noble effort to help individuals live more like Jesus in the "spiritual" aspects of our personal lives, many books have been written on subjects like "how to pray like Jesus," "how to love like Jesus," etc.

Accepting him as a religious figure is easy, but why is it more difficult to view Jesus as a marketer? Isn't *marketer* a label too common, ordinary, non-religious, and unspiritual to be applied to Jesus? It is hard to imagine Jesus engaging in "human" and "worldly" endeavors like marketing. After all, for a large percentage of the world's population, he is considered to be fully God. The Bible says, "For from Him and through Him and to Him are all things" (Romans 11:36). If you believe the Bible, you believe that he created it all. But surely Jesus did not face the types of marketing challenges we face every day in the marketplace of commerce and ideas. Did he?

Yet, Jesus was also fully human. The Bible teaches that Jesus was both fully God and fully man: 100 percent divine and 100 percent human. He was just as human as you and me. As a marketer seeking to influence people strategically, he felt the pain of rejection. He felt the joy of getting his point across, seeing a life changed, and knowing that people were buying into his message.

Everywhere he went, Jesus presented a fork in the road for people, obligating them to make a choice. People would never be the same after meeting him. Throughout the recorded events of his life, he sought specific responses to his invitation. That imperative invitation was this: "follow me."

He invited professional fishermen to drop their nets and follow him.

He invited a rich young ruler to sell all his possessions, give the proceeds to the poor, and follow him.

He invited large groups of people to leave their closest family members to follow him.

Not only was Jesus interested in marketing this invitation to humanity, but it was also his entire purpose for coming to Earth. According to the Bible, he descended from Heaven to Earth to bring a message—a message of love, hope, and freedom. He was the "word" that "became flesh and dwelt among us" (John 1:14). The entire purpose for his life was to deliver a message, the message about himself, to humanity. He *was* the message he came to broadcast to the world. He came to influence in a laser-specific, strategic way. He came as a marketer. As such, he demanded a response from the world. As far as Jesus was concerned, there were only two things a person could do with him: follow him wholeheartedly or reject him completely. There was no middle ground. Either way, a response was required.

You might say, "Well, Jesus wasn't selling anything, so how could he be a *marketer*?" Forget about flash sales and Black Friday discounts on what Jesus was offering. The price to accept his message costs far more than what you paid for this book in your hand. The price to truly accept his message and to follow him? Everything. His life. The follower's life. Costly. Valuable. Demanding. Jesus was marketing an invitation to an exchanged life: the good, bad, and ugly of the recipient's life in exchange for Jesus' flawless life.

How did Jesus deliver this incredibly demanding message while gaining global acceptance throughout history? What can we learn from the life and legacy of Jesus about how to be great marketers—that is, strategic influencers and intentional leaders? Regardless of our profession, how can we influence people the way Jesus influenced them to make a positive impact on the world?

MARKETERS AND MANIPULATORS

If you struggle with not wanting to label Jesus as a "marketer" — or, with labeling yourself as a "marketer" — you are not alone. We have all had bad experiences with selfish, manipulative marketers in business, politics, and even in churches and other nonprofits. Most of us like the marketplace of commerce and ideas. But for most of us, it is the marketers with whom we have a problem.

When I was trying to start my first business, I made a multitude of mistakes. To name one, I hired an unqualified web developer and paid him in advance. I was in a rush to get a fancy e-commerce website built for my new health and fitness services marketing company. For the level of programming work I needed (or, thought I needed), I received several quotes from reputable web developers in the range of $25,000 to build the initial website. Considering I was a business school student at the time, this was out of my price range.

In my search for a less-expensive option, I was referred to a web developer who had a website similar to the one I needed. His site was built for a different industry than mine. He said he could retrofit his website to the specifications I needed for a $5,000 licensing fee. Inexperienced and rash, I paid the money.

As it turned out, he couldn't actually build a website remotely close to what I needed, nor was he willing to hire someone qualified to build it. I waited for my website for six months, hoping this person could deliver on what he promised. Once he confessed to me that he couldn't and wouldn't deliver, he promptly quit responding to my requests for a refund.

Rather than spending more money, time, and energy to go to small claims court, I just forgave the guy and accepted that I had just paid $5,000 in stupid tax to a dishonest marketer. (In business, you sometimes must forgive with zeroes on the end.)

As is often the case with scenarios like this one, that negative experience turned out to be a blessing in disguise. When the web development plan crumbled for my health and fitness website, I decided to learn how to build the website myself. As I learned how to build a basic website, I discovered that I was not as passionate about my new business concept as I thought I was. I promptly applied my newly acquired skills toward building two websites for the purpose of promoting the work of thought leaders, which is the work I am doing today with *Marketing Like Jesus*, the Theology of Business Institute, and as the CEO of a publishing company called High Bridge Books.

Have you had an experience with a bad marketer, one who was entirely self-serving? I will bet you have. Maybe it was a business professional. A religious leader. A political leader. If you are like me, it probably made you more cautious about trusting marketers.

It would be easy to allow the stigma associated with marketers to discourage us from promoting anything. And for those of us who hold Jesus in the highest regard, it would certainly be difficult to categorize him as a marketer because of the bad ones out there trying to manipulate and exploit people.

Every marketer faces the temptation to over-promise and under-deliver. In many cases, the marketer knows perfectly well that he cannot deliver on his promise even if he wants to. He or she makes the promise anyway to get the vote, get the sale, get the member, get the donation, get the favor, or get the follower.

WE NEED A NEW MARKETING ROLE MODEL

It is little wonder why most people try to avoid marketers and try to escape from being labeled as a marketer. We don't want people to assume we're manipulating them. Likewise, we don't want to feel the guilt and condemnation of feeling like we're manipulating people. Nobody wants to be labeled as "pushy" or "self-righteous" for trying to get people to adopt their cause, visit their church, or vote for their candidate. Nobody wants to be labeled "money hungry" or "greedy" just for trying to get people to purchase their product, subscribe to their service, or donate to their charity.

Meanwhile, we are rendered silent and unproductive by this self-defeating, self-sabotaging condemnation that we allow to be placed on ourselves. Our silence keeps us from doing work that is fulfilling, improving the lives of people, and making a positive change in the world. It is easier to remain a passive member of society. It is easier not to promote proactively anything in life. It is more convenient to sit back and criticize those who are actually promoting something.

Indeed, nothing is more challenging than marketing. Getting an idea embedded into your own mind can be tough. Getting that idea into the minds of others is far more difficult. At the same time, it can be extremely fulfilling and rewarding to help others benefit from what you have to offer.

Most of us appreciate the idea of the famous historical figure who passionately proclaimed his message in the face of persecution. We envision romanticized images of the entrepreneur who hustled to make her product or service successful in the marketplace, having overcome all the odds and rejections. Sure, we like the marketplace of commerce and ideas. Most of us value the free exchange of thoughts, goods, and services. Though, the marketers who promote these things are often resented by society. (At the same time, they usually end up being considered society's greatest success stories.) If we are honest, many of us consider marketing to be a necessary evil. Many view marketing as the "dark side" of the private, public, and social sectors.

Yet, anyone responsible for an organization's bottom line knows that nothing happens without marketers. Legendary management expert Peter Drucker said, "The only two functions that count are marketing and innovation. All others are costs." Nothing happens in the world until somebody markets an idea, first to oneself and then to others. If we do not become better marketers, we are robbing the world of the opportunity to benefit from our products, services, messages, and causes.

To become better marketers—strategic influencers and intentional leaders—we need a new model of what a "marketer" is and can be. That model is Jesus Christ. Good marketers market like Jesus; bad marketers don't. Jesus is the most effective marketer of all time, so it makes good sense to follow his example if you want to influence people for a better world.

---

[1] Leonard Sweet and Frank Voila, *Jesus: A Theography* (Nashville: Thomas Nelson, 2012), 104.

[2] Central Intelligence Agency of the United States of America, *The World Factbook*, (2010 estimates), https://www.cia.gov/library/publications/the-world-factbook/geos/xx.html (accessed July 26, 2014).

[3] Timothy Keller, *Jesus the King* (New York: Riverhead, 2011), 134.

[4] Philip Jenkins, *The Next Christendom: The Coming of Global Christianity*. 3rd ed. Vol. 3, Future of Christianity Trilogy (New York: Oxford University Press, 2011), 275.

[5] Scot McKnight, *The Jesus Creed* (Brewster, MA: Paraclete Press, 2004), 227.

[6] Russell Ash, *The Top 10 of Everything, 1997* (New York: DK, 1996), 112.

[7] John Ortberg, Who Is This Man: *The Unpredictable Impact of the Inescapable Jesus* (Grand Rapids: Zondervan, 2012), 62.

[8] Franklin Foer, "Baptism by Celluloid," *The New York Times*, February 8, 2004, http://www.nytimes.com/2004/02/08/movies/baptism-by-celluloid.html.

[9] Leonard Sweet and Frank Voila, *Jesus: A Theography* (Nashville: Thomas Nelson, 2012), x.

SERVE

"What do you want me to do for you?"
Jesus (from Mark 10:35)

TRANSCEND DEAD TRADITIONS

When jets and trucks began to dominate the transportation industry in the 1960s and 1970s, railroad companies declined rapidly. While this may seem like a logical consequence of the new advents in transportation at this time—such as commercial flight and the interstate highway system—it was the railroad companies that were in the best position to take advantage of these trends in the transportation industry. They knew transportation better than any of these new trucking and airline companies. They should have led the shift instead of getting punished by it.

As Theodore Levitt pointed out in his article, "Marketing Myopia,"[1] the heads of these railroad companies mistakenly assumed that they were in the *railroad* industry when they were actually operating within the *transportation* industry. Because of their myopic thinking, they were focused more on gaining market share from their fellow railroad companies than they were on meeting their customers' needs. Their customers just wanted transportation as quickly and efficiently as they could get it. They did not necessarily need railroads to fulfill this need.

Jesus knew that one must be willing to transcend dead traditions to meet people's needs effectively. When Jesus began his three-year marketing campaign, he was faced with a tremendous amount of opposition from a group known as the Pharisees. The Pharisees were among the most highly educated teachers of the Law of Moses, which made them some of the most popular celebrities and powerbrokers in their communities. Many of them allowed their popularity to swell their arrogance. They created a self-serving competition out of conformity to these religious laws. Because they attended the best schools and were the most highly educated about these laws, this manmade competition was rigged in their favor. While Jesus highly respected the Mosaic Law they were seeking to keep—in fact, he came to fulfill it—he transcended their myopic, self-centered, and unjust applications of the Law.

For example, the Pharisees ridiculed Jesus for helping people on the Sabbath Day, the day of the week on which no work was to be performed. Yet, Jesus helped people on the Sabbath anyway, saying, "The Sabbath was made to meet the needs of people, and not people to meet the requirements of the Sabbath" (Mark 2:27, NLT).

Jesus transcended selfish interpretations of the Law. He used this type of phrasing repeatedly: "You have heard it was said... but I say to you..." and "I tell you the truth..." These were introductory statements that he followed up with corrected interpretations and applications of the Law. This Law was established to serve people—not the other way around.

To market his message effectively, Jesus had to transcend dead traditions that were not helping people. Jesus let self-centered powerbrokers know that their unethical practices would no longer go unchecked. He aimed to restore a system of justice and righteousness in his community—and throughout the world—that was not based on outward appearances and behaviors. It was focused first on the condition of a person's heart. He threatened the status quo, which won the allegiance of the outcasts, while enraging the wealthy and powerful. For these reasons, his enemies attempted to discredit him with statements such as,

"He's deceptive."
"He's a glutton and a drunkard."
"He's a blasphemer."
"He was born as the result of fornication."
"He's a false prophet."
"Satan is working through Him!"

These Pharisaical attitudes are present in every industry. It is the attitude that says, "We do it *that* way because it's always been done *that* way." Your industry needs Jesus-like courage and fresh approaches from you to transcend its dead traditions.

As the founder and CEO of a publishing company, I recognize the need to transcend some of the dead traditions in my own industry. There are still many people in the publishing industry who have downright snooty attitudes toward any form of book publishing outside of the "traditional" book deal. *(In a "traditional" book deal, the author usually gets an advance payment to write the book, the publisher absorbs some portion of the costs, and the author gets approximately eight percent of each sale.)* While this attitude is dying with the advent of author-driven publishing, digital publishing, niche publishing, and print-on-demand, there are still those who would say, "If you didn't get a 'traditional' book deal, you can't say that you're a 'published author.'" This logic would be like saying to an entrepreneur, "If you started a company but didn't get a venture capitalist to invest in your company, you can't say that you're a 'true entrepreneur.'" *(Those of us who built our companies with zero outside investment or loans know better.)* Most readers do not know and do not care how the book was published or who published it; they just want to read a good book. In many cases, today's authors can serve their readers better through bypassing "traditional" publishing arrangements in which they must surrender nearly all their royalties to their publishers.

When organizations derail, it is often because they have lost sight of people's needs, focusing instead on preserving their own traditions and investments. Especially when the movement is laced with immorality and poor stewardship, the greatest enemy of the present movement in a society or organization is often the previous movement. Because the bastions of yesteryear's methods often have a great deal invested in old structures and paradigms, things continue to be done the same way because they have always been done that way—even when they take advantage of people or waste resources.

What dead traditions do you need to start transcending in your industry to serve people more effectively? In your community? In your nation? In the world?

---

[1] Theodore Levitt, "Marketing Myopia," *Harvard Business Review* (1960).

AIM TO BE A RESTORER, NOT A RADICAL

When I was 26, I was $26,000 in debt: student loans, an auto loan, credit card debt, and even a loan to buy an expensive Taylor guitar. During that time, I read a book by Dave Ramsey titled *Total Money Makeover*. Though I had made almost no progress toward paying off my debt prior to reading Dave's book, I paid off my $26,000 debt entirely within 12 months after reading it. Why?

As I read Dave's plan for becoming debt-free and building wealth, I began to experience a mindset shift in how I had been thinking about money. It became clear to me that Dave's goal in marketing his financial plan isn't to offer a flashy new "get-rich-quick" scheme. Instead, his goal has been to help people apply ancient, time-tested, Biblical principles about money to restore what many people have lost or never discovered in the first place: financial peace and financial freedom.

Jesus said about his mission, "The son of man has come to seek and to save that which was lost" (Luke 19:10). This mission of Jesus is highlighted in Luke 15 when he told three consecutive parables about a "lost sheep," "lost coin," and a "lost son" that each became found. He was more interested in restoration than revolution. Society had fallen so far off-course that his coming felt like a radical revolution. Rather than marketing something as altogether new, Jesus declared that his mission was to "seek and to save that which was lost" to reestablish the relationship that had been severed between God and humanity, a relationship as ancient as Creation itself. Rather than marketing his ideals as something radically new and progressive, Jesus aimed to restore something ancient, timeless, and transcendent beyond the world's systems.

Radicals despise things that are not "new" and "progressive." Marketing like Jesus isn't about promoting "the next big thing." It's not about trying to develop the next "disruptive" innovation or idea to overthrow competitors in your industry.

Like Jesus, we should aim to restore through our marketing rather than aiming merely to revolt against something or conquer something. Restorers focus on finding solutions rather than on merely shouting about the problems. Especially when aiming to correct something that has deviated so far away from meeting people's needs, our marketing as restorers may appear like we are doing something radical and revolutionary. However, do not give into society's temptation to pursue change merely for the sake of change. What may appear to be "progress" may actually be a digression.

As restorers rather than radicals, some marketers aim to provide remedies for human illnesses or illiteracy. Some serve to fill gaps in customer service. Some focus on restoring human dignity where it seems to have been degraded.

Others promote the opportunity to experience greater happiness and fulfillment in life. In every case, marketers who influence like Jesus will restore what humanity is lacking or has lost altogether. Marketers who aim to be radicals and disruptors, pursuing change for the sake of change, will continue contributing to the lack and lostness.

Is the aim of your marketing primarily to start a revolution or to cause restoration?

In your industry and/or society, what is lost that needs to be found again?

FIND A NEED AND FILL IT

Based on their research, psychologists at Yale University determined that the most persuasive words in the English language are "discovery, guarantee, love, new, results, save, easy, health, money, proven, safety, and you."[1] These words are persuasive because they connect with deep human needs. That is why they have become the focus of the most effective advertisements and commercials we see. Charles Revson, founder of Revlon cosmetics, said, "In the factories we make perfume, but in the stores we sell hope." Organizations collectively spend billions on advertisements that promise fulfillment, success, happiness, and other intangible products that money cannot buy. Their advertisers know that people are loyal to companies they feel have improved their lives in some way.

Jesus never turned a person away in his or her time of need. He did not always give them exactly what they asked for, but he always met their need in some way, often targeting both the person's tangible and intangible needs.

The Gospels—*Matthew, Mark, Luke,* and *John*—record 35 accounts of people who received healing from Jesus. He probably healed hundreds or even thousands more to demonstrate his message of hope.

He met people's vocational needs. When he told fishermen—Peter, James, and John—where to drop their nets despite the improbable odds they would catch anything, they caught more fish than their nets could hold.

He served people by teaching them the principles that undergird a life well-lived.

He met people's needs for affirmation and approval. Even when his disciples were debating who among them would be the greatest in heaven, Jesus did not say, "Guys, you are vain and selfish. You shouldn't be having this conversation." Instead, knowing they had a deep need for significance and that increasing their influence was necessary for spreading his message, Jesus taught them how to be great: "be last of all and servant of all" (Mark 9:35). In other words, "Find a need and fill it." While Jesus always targeted the deeper layer of need in a person's life, he did not disregard even their most superficial requests because there was always a deeper need beneath the surface.

Ultimately, Jesus demonstrated the ultimate act of service by dying the worst death imaginable as a pardon for every way in which we have offended our Creator.

Jesus made himself available to meeting needs, which gave him more insight into what people needed. He was not marketing miracles and good deeds. He was marketing transformed lives, which cost people everything to experience. He was in the life-changing business.

Marketers often think, "If I could just get my prospects to understand what I'm offering ... then, they would want it." Yet, understanding the description of a product is not enough to engage a prospect. Rather than focusing on the features of your product or service, you must direct your message toward the deeper need, your prospect's underlying desire. You must target the desires of your prospect to get him or her to engage. Like Jesus, you must connect with a deeply felt human need, which triggers that desire for what you are offering.

Most marketers can easily describe what their product or service is. Most can help people understand what the product can do. However, that is where many of us stop. Marketers often fail to explain specifically the outcome of how their product or service can improve someone's life.

If the miraculous signs and wonders people saw were not enough for Jesus to turn someone into a believer, we certainly cannot rely on flashy features, persuasive words, and thorough product demonstrations to market effectively. We must always target people's deeper needs, aiming to serve them in the most meaningful ways possible. More than appealing to their understanding, we must target their desires. As the sales axiom goes, "Sell the hole, not the drill." A person buys a drill not merely to have an extra appliance around the house. She buys it for the holes it can make that will help to improve her life somehow (e.g., hanging a beautiful picture, etc.). By focusing on what people need deep down, not merely on the features of your product or service, people will begin to see the tremendous value you are creating.

As a marketer, what is the deep human need you are trying to meet? Once you have an answer to this question, ask yourself, "Why would someone want this?" Repeat this process until you have identified the fundamental human need you are aiming to fulfill.

---

[1] Jay Conrad Levinson, *Guerrilla Marketing* (Boston: Houghton Mifflin, 2007), 145.

SERVE: STRATEGY 4

BE GENEROUS

According to some studies, "free" is the most powerful word in marketing. With so many different options in today's marketplaces of commerce and ideas, allowing people to test what you are offering before they commit is usually mandatory. Many internet companies use a "freemium" business model, which allows people to subscribe to a basic version of their online service with the hope that the users will eventually upgrade to a paid version of the service. Venture capitalists invest in these companies often under the assumption that only six percent of the users will actually subscribe to a paid version of the service. If the paying customers had not originally been part of the 94 percent that enjoyed free service, they probably would not have become paying customers.

Long before "free" became a buzzword in today's marketplace, Jesus offered services for "free," services that cost the recipient little but cost him everything. He told the story of ten lepers who were healed of their leprosy in which only one out of the ten returned to express his gratitude (Luke 17:11-19). Although Jesus knew that most people would not be willing to commit their lives to being his followers, he continued to allow people to benefit from his services. When a person requested a service from Jesus, such as a healing, he did not respond, "I will only heal you if you contribute money toward my cause and start spreading my message to your friends and family." No, he gave freely. Yes, Jesus wanted people to become his followers, but he was extravagantly generous toward them, regardless of how they responded. Frequently, people did not even appreciate what Jesus had done for them, but he served them anyway. This was always Jesus' attitude: "What do you want me to do for you?" (Mark 10:35)

Generosity is essential for building a relationship with potential advocates of your brand. Tylenol supplies free pain relievers for competitors at skateboarding competitions, and they do not post signs about it. They just provide a service to the kids, and word-of-mouth about their product spreads organically. Word-of-mouth marketing expert Andy Sernovitz says, "Treat people well, and they will do your marketing for you, for free." As a marketer, you can surge in effectiveness by offering valuable products, services, and content at no cost to potential advocates of your brand. Let people taste and see. Give. Give. Give. Then, ask for something. (Yes, do not forget to ask!)

What valuable products, services, or content could you offer for free to potential advocates of your brand that would incline them to become ambassadors for your brand?

OFFER RESULTS FOR EVERY CLAIM

When I was taking MBA courses in New York City, I had a plan for a new business venture which I entered into my university's annual new business venture pitch contest. My idea was to launch a website where people could shop for health and fitness services in their local areas (i.e. gym memberships, exercise classes, etc.). The concept was at least good enough to become a finalist in the contest that year.

After I gave my three-minute pitch, I felt okay about it. I had explained the concept and how I believed people would use it. However, the investors primarily wanted to know one thing: "What results have you achieved so far?" Huh? I had spent so much time in business school learning about writing a business plan and doing financial projections that I had not spent time creating a prototype and actually getting people to try my service. I was focused on theory; the investors were focused on results. The team that won had already generated $10,000 from their idea.

While his opponents were focused on promoting their opinions and theories, Jesus was always focused on results. While they emphasized form, Jesus emphasized substance.

To illustrate the primacy of results over claims, outcomes over promises, Jesus told a parable about two sons:

> But what do you think? A man had two sons, and he came to the first and said, "Son, go work today in the vineyard." And he answered, "I will not"; but afterward he regretted it and went. The man came to the second and said the same thing; and he answered, "I will, sir"; but he did not go. Which of the two did the will of his father? (Matt. 21:28-32)

Obviously, the one that went to work in the vineyard was the one who *did* what he was supposed to do. He under-promised and over-delivered while his brother did nothing more than lie. Only one of them generated results.

While sitting downcast in prison for challenging wickedness in the government, John the Baptist sent a message to Jesus, asking him, "Are You the Expected One, or shall we look for someone else?" (Matthew 11:3) In that moment, John lapsed from being Jesus' chief promoter to questioning whether it was all just a hoax. Even John the Baptist, the one who prepared the way for Jesus' public ministry, experienced a moment of extreme weakness in which he doubted Jesus' message. John had given his entire life to preparing people to receive their heavenly King, the Messiah, the one who would deliver his people from centuries of bondage. He was the one to declare that Jesus was the Messiah, the Lamb of God who would die to save the world. He was the last person one might expect to doubt Jesus' message.

Rather than abandoning John for his moment of doubt and frustration, Jesus had compassion on him and addressed his concern. Pointing John's attention toward the results of Jesus' ministry, Jesus told his messengers,

> Go and report to John what you hear and see: the blind receive sight and the lame walk, the lepers are cleansed and the deaf hear, the dead are raised up, and the poor have the gospel preached to them. (Matt. 11:4-5)

Jesus overcame John's objections with empirical proof. He gave John results—not claims only. He was doing all the things he said he was going to do in his mission statement (stated in Luke 4:18-19).

People gave Jesus all kinds of excuses for why they would not accept his message. Either they would not accept him at all, would not accept him now, or refused to accept him any longer. With 35 healings recorded in the Gospels, a life that was above reproach, and countless transformed lives, Jesus addressed their concerns with results—not claims alone.

Jesus taught, "For each tree is known by its own fruit" (Luke 6:44a). In other words, a person's claims are secondary to what they actually produce. To market like Jesus, overcome people's objections and indifference with results—not opinions and theories. Especially in the Information Age, people are overwhelmed with opinions and theories. Results to support claims are scarce. People may listen to opinions, but they usually won't change their behavior because of opinions. No matter what you are marketing or to whom you're marketing, you will encounter objections, so you must be able to demonstrate how your ideas have already generated the results people desire.

Do not advertise your aspirations. Advertise the truth. The truth is found in the results—not opinions. Your success will come not from what you promise but from what you deliver.

What proof (e.g., statistics, testimonials, etc.) do you have that your products, services, and/or ideas are generating the results you have promised?

Are there any areas in your marketing where you do not have evidence to support the promises you are making? What changes do you need to make?

FUNCTION 2

TARGET

"He who has ears to hear, let him hear."
Jesus (from Mark 4:9)

TARGET: STRATEGY 6

DEFINE YOUR TARGET GROUP

In 2003, Hillary Clinton's memoir sold more than 200,000 copies per month for three months. That year, *USA Today* mistakenly named her as the best-selling nonfiction author in the United States. During the same period, a little-known Baptist pastor named Rick Warren published a book titled *The Purpose Driven Life*, which sold one million copies per month for 18 months following its release. Warren accomplished this without any national advertising or publicity. It sold 30 million copies in three years, making it the fastest-selling hardcover book in history.[1] How was this possible?

Ten years before most of us first heard of Rick Warren, he wrote a book to help pastors titled *The Purpose Driven Church*. To continue building relationships with pastors, he served them by providing free online resources at www.pastors.com, including an exceptional podcast I benefitted from regularly. As a result of targeting and serving pastors, Warren's list grew to 85,000 pastors who wanted to keep receiving leadership guidance from him. Greg Stielstra, co-author of the book *Faith-Based Marketing*, who managed the targeted marketing campaign for *The Purpose Driven Life*, writes,

> [Rick Warren] offered *Purpose Driven Life* to [the 85,000 pastors on his list] for $7 (normally $20) if they would conduct a 40-day campaign in their churches. He sent a single e-mail to his list and 1,200 churches agreed to participate. The pastors were asked to preach six sermons based on the six sections of the book. Each member would also buy the $20 book for just $7 and commit to reading a chapter a day for 40 days. Finally, small groups in each church met in homes to discuss the book during this 40-day campaign. Members of the participating churches immediately bought 400,000 copies, though at barely a breakeven price for the publisher. The publisher expected 100,000 first year sales. Retailers wondered if anyone would purchase the book for $20 when they could get it at $7. Within two months, those 400,000 consumer evangelists produced two million copies sold.[2]

As a young man, I remember sticking around after church one day to attend an information session about starting a *Purpose Driven Life* discussion group. Later that week, my college roommate and I started having guys over to our dorm room to discuss the book. The book made a profound impact on me, but it was primarily my pastor's recommendation that motivated me to start a discussion group about the book. This may have never happened if

Rick Warren had not faithfully and consistently defined and served his target group, which included my pastor.

While Jesus' mission was to reach the entire world with his message, He first focused on serving a specific group of people during the three years of his ministry on earth: the Jewish people. The Apostle Paul explained that Jesus' message came to the Jewish people first:

> For I am not ashamed of the gospel, for it is the power of God for salvation to everyone who believes, *to the Jew first* and also to the Greek.
> (Rom. 1:16, emphasis mine)

When a non-Jewish woman asked Jesus to heal her demon-possessed daughter, Jesus responded, "I was sent only to the lost sheep of *the house of Israel*" (Matthew 15:24, emphasis mine). Though Jesus had compassion on this Gentile woman and served her, he reminded her that she was not part of his target group. When she implored him to help her and her daughter, Jesus said, "It is not good to take the children's bread and throw it to the dogs" (Matthew 15:26). Scot McKnight, author of *The Jesus Creed*, explains,

> Jesus challenges her faith with a riddle. Jesus says: "Let the children of Israel eat from the kingdom table first. Wait your turn." Not to be denied even by Jesus, the woman pulls a remarkable twist out of her own bag of riddles: "Even the dogs [Jewish code word for Gentiles] eat the crumbs that fall from their Master's table." Challenge met again.[3]

James Edwards observed, "The Samaritan woman answered Jesus from within the parable."[4] The Samaritan woman understood that the gospel message was ultimately for everybody, but she also understood that Jesus was focused primarily on sharing his message with the Jewish people during his ministry. Seeing she understood that the gospel was for everyone in the world, Jesus responded, "O woman, your faith is great; it shall be done for you as you wish" (Matt. 15:28).

Not only did Jesus target his message toward a specific ethnic group and nationality, the Jewish people in Israel, he targeted a specific subgroup among the Jewish people: the outcasts. Jesus said of his ministry on earth, "I have come to the *lost sheep* of the house of Israel" (Matthew 15:24, emphasis mine). These "lost sheep" were the despised and outcast members of Israel's society, "the tax collectors and the sinners." Everything he said and did was said and done with this specific group in mind.

When Jesus invited Matthew to become one of his 12 closest disciples, Matthew held one of the most despised occupations in all of Israel—he was a Jewish tax collector. Tax collectors were usually affluent Jewish people who, in effect, bought the franchise rights to tax their own people on behalf of the Roman government. As long as they gave Caesar his share, they could charge their fellow Jews whatever they wanted. As a despised outcast among the Jewish people, Matthew was exactly the type of person Jesus wanted to follow him. The Bible says that Matthew

… invited Jesus and his disciples to his home as dinner guests, along with many tax collectors and other disreputable sinners. (There were *many people of this kind* among Jesus' followers.) (Mark 2:15, emphasis mine)

During his public ministry, Jesus did not target Israel's best and brightest. He did not go after the pillars of the community. Wayward as they were, he targeted the "disreputable sinners" who epitomized the "lost sheep of the house of Israel." Insignificant as they were, these "lost sheep" were the ones who spread Jesus' message around the world.

Jesus' marketing strategy can be compared to the process of starting a wildfire. To start a wildfire, one does not light 100 matches and scatter them in random places. Instead, one needs to ignite and fan a flame upon a single, small pile of kindling wood. It may take a while to enflame the kindling, but the fire will spread by itself once that job is done. For Jesus, the lost sheep of the house of Israel were the kindling who spread his message throughout the world.

As a book publisher, I have worked with many people who are afraid to target their message toward a specific group. Many of us fear that we would be "limiting" our impact by targeting a specific group. After all, wouldn't we reach a larger audience if we try to reach "everybody"? No, that is a myth rooted in fear. Ironically, products and services marketed to "everybody" usually reach very few people.

First, not everybody wants what you're offering. Second, you do not have the resources to reach "everybody" — at least, initially.

With all the noise of the Information Age competing for your prospects' attention, it has never been more important to ensure that your message is targeted toward a specific, niche group of people. Today, most forms of media are available on-demand, so people can now pay attention to exactly what they want, when they want. If something is not oriented specifically for them, they are likely to ignore it.

Yes, have a massive vision, but also aim for a small target within the scope of your overall vision. Zig Ziglar said, "If you aim at nothing, you will hit it every time." If you are marketing something, you need a target group. Your influence will grow as you become more specific about who you are targeting.

In my case, I am uniquely gifted to serve thought leaders seeking to demonstrate their Christian faith in the marketplace of commerce and ideas. Naturally, this is my target group. The *Marketing Like Jesus* book and the *Theology of Business Podcast* were created specifically for this type of person, and my publishing company mostly publishes books written by these types of people.

What type of person are you uniquely gifted to serve? Give this person a name. Where does he/she live? How old is he/she? What does he/she do for a living? How does he/she think? What motivates him/her? What are his/her needs?

[1] Bob Hutchins and Greg Stielstra, *Faith-Based Marketing* (Hoboken: Wiley, 2009), 85.

[2] Ibid.

[3] Scot McKnight, *The Jesus Creed* (Brewster, MA: Paraclete Press, 2004), 189.

[4] Timothy Keller, *Jesus the King* (New York: Riverhead, 2011), 97.

START WITH THOSE WHO ARE HUNGRY

Mel Gibson had already spent $20 million of his own money to make the film *The Passion of the Christ*, so his advertising budget was limited. To ensure that none of his promotion budget was wasted, he wanted to target his efforts as carefully as possible. He did not merely ask himself, "How can I tell as many people about this movie as possible?" To target his efforts, he reframed the question as, "Who would be most likely to want to see a movie about the suffering, death, and resurrection of Jesus Christ?"

Gibson decided that evangelical pastors would be the right group to target as they are always looking for ways to communicate the gospel in a profound way. Bob Hutchins, who led the marketing campaign for the film, writes,

> [Mel Gibson] began inviting pastors to private screenings of the film, even before it was complete. Initially, he showed it to a fairly small groups of pastors—10 to 12 at a time. A month prior to the release, he was showing it to 5,000 pastors at a time. At Willow Creek, Bill Hybels

asked him after moments of silence, "Alright, what do you need us to do?" They began urging their congregations to see it, and even provided bus transportation.[1]

I remember winning two tickets to the movie in a drawing at a Christian event on my college campus. The tickets were donated on the condition that the winner would bring someone to the movie who was not a Christian—which is exactly what I did.

Jesus said, "It is not those who are healthy who need a physician, but those who are sick" (Mark 2:17a). He did not waste his time trying to make people dissatisfied without him. Instead, he focused his time on offering solutions to people who recognized their desperation for what he was offering. Yes, Jesus loved everybody, but he was focused concerning his overall marketing strategy. He pursued the outcasts, those who realized their need for him and his message. Leonard Sweet writes,

> It is clear from the Gospels that Jesus' main audience was never the religious leaders. Jesus wasn't trying to persuade or convert the Jewish establishment. Exceptions, like Nicodemus (and probably Joseph of Arimathea), came to Jesus. But Jesus was addressing the common people who gave Him a hearing. Thus He kept to the villages, staying away from the large Galilean towns, like Sepphoris and Tiberias. Interestingly, the Gospels don't mention these two cities, which were the largest in Galilee.[2]

He did not waste time with people who did not recognize their need for what he was offering. When Jesus sent his disciples out to share his message, he told them, "Whoever does not receive you, nor heed your words, as you go out of that house or that city, shake the dust off your feet" (Matthew 10:14). This was not a pompous, "some-will-some-won't-so-what" attitude toward those who rejected what he was offering. He loved them, blessed them, and called his followers to do the same. He simply did not want them wasting their time with those who were not hungry for what they had to offer. He told his audiences, "He who has ears to hear, let him hear" (Mark 4:9). In other words, "My message is for those hungry for my solution."

Approximately 10 percent of the people who hear your message will probably despise you and what you are offering.

Another 80 percent of the people you contact simply won't care about you or what you are offering.

The remaining 10 percent of the people who hear your message will love what you are offering. They will be your raving fans. They might even grow to love it more than you do. That is where you need to focus at least 80 percent of your time and attention.

What type of person is the hungriest for what you have to offer?

Are you spending at least 80 percent of your time with those who are hungry for your solution?

[1] Bob Hutchins and Greg Stielstra, *Faith-Based Marketing* (Hoboken: Wiley, 2009), 87.

[2] Leonard Sweet and Frank Voila, *Jesus: A Theography* (Nashville: Thomas Nelson, 2012), 104.

BECOME AN EXPERT ON YOUR TARGET GROUP

Feeling that they needed to reinvent their brand to stay ahead of Pepsi, executives at the Coca-Cola Company decided to introduce a newer and sweeter version of Coca-Cola. This "New Coke" was intended to replace the original version.

In taste tests, 55 percent to 45 percent preferred New Coke over the old one. But when the product came to market, Coca-Cola's fans revolted when they discovered that their beloved Coca-Cola was being supplanted by the newer, albeit tastier version. Sergio Zyman, who was Coke's chief marketing officer at the time of New Coke, explained,

> We did not know enough about our consumers. We did not even know what motivated them to buy Coke in the first place. We fell into the trap of imagining that innovation—abandoning our existing product for a new one—would cure our ills.[1]

Donald Keough, then president of the Coca-Cola Company, said about consumers' diehard loyalty to the original Coke, "It's a wonderful American mystery, a lovely American enigma. And you can't measure it any more than you can measure love, pride, or patriotism."[2]

The lesson from this classic example is clear: become an expert on your target group. In marketing, do not do things simply because the competition is doing it. Instead, focus on learning more about the deep needs of the target group you are supposed to be serving.

Jesus frequently surprised people when they found out how well he knew them. One day, Phillip enthusiastically invited his brother, Nathanael, to come and meet Jesus. Skeptically, Nathanael replied, "Can any good thing come out of Nazareth?" (John 1:46a)

The Bible says that, when Jesus saw Nathanael coming, he said, "Behold, an Israelite indeed, in whom there is no deceit!" (John 1:47)

Confused, Nathanael replied, "How do You know me?" (John 1:48a)

Jesus responded, "Before Philip called you, when you were under the fig tree, I saw you" (John 1:48b).

Astonished that Jesus knew so much about him, Nathanael said, "Rabbi, You are the Son of God; You are the King of Israel" (John 1:49).

Jesus was always studying his target group to know them better. He wanted to know everything about them. As was the case with his 12 disciples, he studied them and selected them before they decided to follow him. He told them, "You did not choose Me but I chose you, and appointed you that you would go and bear fruit" (John 15:16a). Jesus did his research on these guys before he ever asked them for a commitment. Like Jesus, we should know our target group so well that our members, customers, followers, constituents, donors, and clients feel as though they were pre-selected and hand-picked to join us.

The most successful marketers take this principle of "become an expert on your target group" very seriously. When you understand the traits of your audience, you can import those traits into your brand. For example, products and services aimed at men tend to emphasize specifications and numbers (i.e. Ford's F-150 truck, Gillette's Mach-3 razor, PS4, etc). (*I will not pontificate here on whether men prefer these types of labels more than women, but this is certainly the view taken by many of today's advertisers—at least, in practice.*)

Wal-Mart maintains a 7.5-terabyte database of information about their customers' buying habits, which is many times the size of the federal government's database of people's personal information. As a result, Wal-Mart has accumulated extremely detailed information about their customers. For example, they discovered that "a shopper who buys a Barbie doll is 60 percent more likely to purchase one of three types of candy bars ... and toothpaste is most often bought alongside canned tuna."[3]

It is impossible to target a group without studying and knowing its members. Without spending time getting to know them, we're left with faulty assumptions about what they want, what they need, and what makes them tick. This is one of the reasons why some Fortune 500 companies require that their salespeople ask at least three nonbusiness questions before discussing business-related matters. You must understand the "person" before you can understand the "client," "member," "constituent," "donor," or "customer."

What percentage of your time do you spend with members of your target group?

What tools do you need to use to learn more about your target group? (e.g., Google Analytics, Facebook Analytics, surveys, etc.)

---

[1] Jay Conrad Levinson, *Guerrilla Marketing* (Boston: Houghton Mifflin, 2007), 84.

[2] Robert B. Cialdini, Noah J. Goldstein, and Steve J. Martin, *Yes! 50 Scientifically Proven Ways to Be Persuasive* (New York: Free Press, 2008), 145.

[3] Martin Lindstrom, *Brandwashed: Tricks Companies Use to Manipulate Our Minds and Persuade Us to Buy* (New York: Crown Business, 2011), 217.

TARGET: STRATEGY 9

AIM SMALL, THINK BIG

In 2006, the CEO of the clothing chain, Abercrombie & Fitch, told the world unabashedly that his company did not want anyone but the "cool and popular kids" shopping in his company's stores. He told a reporter,

> In every school there are the cool and popular kids, and then there are the not-so-cool kids ... Candidly, we go after the cool kids. We go after the attractive all-American kid with a great attitude and a lot of friends. A lot of people don't belong [in our clothes], and they can't belong. Are we exclusionary? Absolutely.[1]

Though Abercrombie & Fitch is now struggling financially, this CEO seemed quite proud of his company's focused "targeting" strategy. Yet, through his statement, he communicated that his company does not care about anyone other than his target group—that is, young, "cool" people. Although it is targeted, it is a myopic vision.

Jesus considered every person as a potential beneficiary of what he was offering—not just his target group of Jewish outcasts. While he focused on serving Jewish outcasts during his three-year public ministry, his vision extended far beyond that. He instructed his disciples to carry his message "to the ends of the earth."

While Jesus had a clear target group, he never refused to serve those outside his target group. Targeting isn't about excluding. As people outside Jesus' target group requested things from him, he never refused to serve them. He offered something for everybody, from the lowest to the highest rungs of society. He did not discriminate against people of any socioeconomic status, age, or ethnicity. Although he was focused regarding how he spent his limited time with people, his vision was too massive to discriminate against anybody.

Jesus exhorted his teams to plant and fertilize the seeds of his message throughout the entire world. He instructed his disciples, "You will be my disciples in Jerusalem, Judea, and to the uttermost parts of the earth" (Acts 1:8). Jesus strategically began his movement in Jerusalem, the place that was most ready for it. The citizens of Jerusalem were the first to learn about the Crucifixion and the Resurrection of Jesus. Jerusalem was to be the epicenter for this worldwide expansion of God's Kingdom, the place where Jesus was crucified and resurrected. Clearly, a mission of this magnitude could only be carried out through having a strong presence of Jesus' followers within every nation, ethnicity, group, and sub-group on the planet. Considering one out of every three people in the world identifies as a Christian, his strategy still seems to be working.

In the mid-1900s, Frank C. Laubach served as a Congregationalist missionary in the Philippines, ministering to the Moros people. He also faced the decision of whether to include all of humanity in his vision for his work. Exasperated, he cried out in prayer, "What can I do for hateful people like these: murderers, thieves, dirty filthy betel nut chewers—our enemies?" He writes,

> My lips began to move and it seemed to me that God was speaking. "My child," my lips said, "you have failed because you do not really love these Moros. You feel superior to them because you are white. If you can forget you are an American and think only how I love them, they will respond."

After enlarging his vision and his heart to bless people who were outside his comfort zone, Laubach became a pioneer in literacy with his plan called "Each One Teach One." His prayer was that everyone who learns to read would teach one more person how to read. He set up literacy programs in more than one hundred countries, 313 languages, and was responsible for teaching over 60 million people to read! He became known as the "Apostle to the Illiterates." This happened because he overcame his own prejudices and embraced a vision that was for the benefit of all humanity—not just for the benefit of a specific group.

Again, targeting is not excluding. If the entire world is not eligible to benefit in some way from what you are offering, your vision is too small. Be sure to think big while you are targeting small.

Is your vision bigger than your target group? Is there anyone or any type of person who cannot benefit—or, who potentially could be negatively affected—by your core message and vision?

---

[1] Benoit Denizet-Lewis, "The Man Behind Abercrombie and Fitch," *Salon* (January 24, 2006), http://www.salon.com/2006/01/24/jeffries/ (accessed July 26, 2014).

FUNCTION 3

CONNECT

"Isn't this the carpenter's son?"
Matthew 13:55

CONNECT: STRATEGY 10

FIND COMMON GROUND

In the mid-1800s, Father Damien De Veuster was serving as a young missionary in the Kingdom of Hawaii. While ministering to people in Oahu, the nation began to experience an outbreak of leprosy, a horrific disease that disfigured and killed hundreds of Hawaiians. Unaware that most people are immune to leprosy, the King of Hawaii approved the "Act to Prevent the Spread of Leprosy" that confined about 8,000 diseased Hawaiians to the island of Molokai.

Father Damien felt a burden to share the message of Jesus Christ with these outcasts of Hawaiian society. He spent 16 years ministering to their physical, emotional, and spiritual needs. He reminded his congregation weekly, "God loves you lepers." Then, one week, he got up and said, "God loves *us* lepers," having contracted leprosy himself. Before dying as a leper, he wrote to his brother, "I make myself a leper with the lepers to gain all to Jesus Christ." In the most sacrificial and humble way possible, Father Damien found common ground with his target group.

With the goal of winning the hearts and minds of Israel's outcasts, Jesus positioned himself as an outcast. He was not educated formally within the system that would lead to prominence within his society. He was an outsider, yet he easily could have chosen a path that would lead to formal authority in his society. He could have become a religious professional—such as a scribe or rabbi—but he chose instead to become part of the working class. He opted to become a blue-collar worker, a craftsman working in his father's business. According to the Greek translation of the Gospels, Jesus was a "tekton" by trade, which refers to someone who works with stone and wood (see Matthew 13:55; Mark 6:3).

Jesus' choice to identify with the Jewish outcasts, his target group, caused him to experience a great deal of ridicule. Although he did not have the credentials that most people required from their religious teachers, he did not back down from sharing his message with authority. Rabbinical scholar David Instone-Brewer said, "He was rejected from the start … He stood out as someone having great authority, but outside the system." People were mystified that such understanding, wisdom, power, and authority could emit from a blue-collar worker who had not been formally taught or ordained by their religious leaders. They asked, "Isn't this the carpenter's son?" (Matthew 13:55) They were saying, "He isn't qualified!" Jesus forfeited his reputation among those he was not targeting to establish common ground with his target group.

In addition to becoming like his target group, he spent almost all his time with them. Tim Keller writes,

> Nothing about Jesus breathes the need for the gymnasium in Tiberias, or the Sanhedrin's audience in Jerusalem, or a daily platform in the

courts of the temple. Nor does he need Rome's theater in Sepphoris.[1]

Instead, he chose to spend his time with his target group in the obscure places—such as the countryside—not on the grand stages of his society. While Jesus did speak in the temple, he shared his message primarily in the fields, in the homes of lowly members of society, and especially in fishing boats.

To establish common ground with those you want to serve, you must become like them to some extent. That is the only way to understand truly how they think, what they need, and what they desire. We can only identify with those we want to serve as we spend time with them. To some extent, the culture of your target group must become a part of your own personal and organizational culture.

To the extent that Jesus targeted the "lost sheep of the house of Israel," we can only target one group effectively. Staying focused on your target group requires discipline. If Jesus would have become a Pharisee to connect with the Pharisees, hoping to change the world as an elite member of his society, he most likely would have lost common ground with the uneducated and lowly members of his Jewish society.

When the Evian bottled water company first began marketing its bottled water in China, it did not achieve much success. The brand soon learned that most of the urban Chinese grew up in the surrounding rural areas and, as a result, preferred to drink water that had more of an earthy taste. In response to what Evian learned about the people they wanted to serve, the company located well water in China that would maintain a "faint, grassy, moldy" taste after filtration.[2] Evian knew that their target group would buy bottled water, but they did not know how the water needed to taste until they spent time with them.

I serve thought leaders—particularly, authors. As the CEO of a publishing company, I have been much more effective in working with authors because I am an author myself. This has made me much more understanding of their struggles, needs, and desires.

Your target group wants to know two things: 1) "Do I want what you have?" and 2) "Can I identify with you?"

In what ways are you trying to find common ground with your target group?

---

[1] Scot McKnight, *The Jesus Creed* (Brewster, MA: Paraclete Press, 2004), 137.

[2] Martin Lindstrom, *Brandwashed: Tricks Companies Use to Manipulate Our Minds and Persuade Us to Buy* (New York: Crown Business, 2011), 152.

KEEP YOUR CORE
MESSAGE SIMPLE

On average, people are inundated with approximately 4,700 marketing messages each day.[1] This is especially true in the United States, which has only six percent of the world's population yet consumes 56 percent of the world's advertising.[2] With this amount of noise, today's marketers must be clear or be ignored. Saying many words usually communicates nothing.

Consider that many of the most memorable writings and speeches in history were also some of the shortest. The Lord's Prayer contains only 56 words; the Gettysburg Address, 266; the Ten Commandments, 297; and the Declaration of Independence, 300. To keep it memorable, keep it simple. As one of my Air Force commanders used to say, "Be clear. Be brief. Be seated."

While his message was mysterious and profound to everyone who heard it, Jesus kept his core message clear:

> The Spirit of the Lord is upon Me, because He anointed Me to preach the gospel to the poor. He has sent Me to proclaim release to the captives, and recovery of sight to the blind, to set free

those who are oppressed, to proclaim the favorable year of the Lord. (Luke 4:18-19)

This was the "good news," the "gospel" (Mark 1:1). Jesus' message was not about rules or complex, high-brow philosophy. His message was not advice; it was news. Clear and concise, Jesus' core message was to inform people that they had been set free from living hopeless and pointless lives. Through a relationship with their Creator, they were now free to experience the inner peace for which they had longed. All they had to do was accept what he offered. Although easier said than done, it was simple.

Further, Jesus communicated his simple message in a brief and concise way. Leonard Sweet writes,

> Jesus was a master of the One-Minute Message. In poetic form, He could have delivered the Sermon on the Mount in less than a minute. In poetic form, the Lord's Prayer can be recited in Hebrew in less than a minute, and almost every parable takes only a minute to tell.[3]

Undoubtedly, Jesus could have held a captive audience as long as anybody. Yet, he chose to keep his message brief and to the point.

Can you explain your core message to someone in one sentence? If you were building a house, that single sentence would be like the foundation of your house upon which everything else is built. It must be solid. Most people and organizations are trying to be "jacks of all trades, masters of none," building all over the place but never finishing anything. When it comes to your foundation, you do not want to be a generalist. When people do not know what you are about, they will quickly give up trying to figure you out and will draw their own incorrect conclusions. The jack-of-all-trades-master-of-none approach—that is, trying to be great at everything for fear of "limiting" ourselves and missing opportunities—does not work in marketing today. You probably have a variety of interests and talents which you should explore; however, people cannot understand or remember you if you do not give them one clear message.

At the same time, people pursue those who know who they are, what they offer, and where they are going. People just need one good and clear reason to follow you. Give them one simple, clearly defined, and brief message to help them understand and remember you.

Famous for getting pizza to their customers in "30 minutes or its free," the devout Christian founder and former president of Domino's Pizza, Tom Monaghan, was asked to share his company's secret to success. His answer? "A fanatical focus on doing one thing well."

For FedEx's shipping services, the brand promise is all about "when it absolutely has to be there overnight."

Second to Hertz, Avis boasts chiefly in their commitment to a higher level of service in their industry, saying, "We're Number Two. We Try Harder."

To help people understand what you are offering, distill your value proposition down to one or two sentences. One phrase is even better.

In one or two sentences max, what is your core marketing message? In other words, what makes you (and/or your organization) one-of-a-kind?

[1] Jay Conrad Levinson, *Guerrilla Marketing* (Boston: Houghton Mifflin, 2007), 133.

[2] Al Ries and Jack Trout, *Positioning: The Battle for Your Mind* (New York: McGraw-Hill, 2001), 13.

[3] Leonard Sweet and Frank Voila, *Jesus: A Theography* (Nashville: Thomas Nelson, 2012), 152.

TAKE CONTROL OF YOUR BRAND

Researchers in the field of neuro-marketing conducted fMRI brain scans on hundreds of people to identify neurological reactions to viewing various brand logos and religious symbols. When the research subjects saw famous logos such as Apple's and Coca-Cola's, the same neurological reactions were triggered as when they viewed religious images such as a cross, the Virgin Mary, a Star of David, or a mosque.[1]

While it may have already been obvious to you, strong brands carry an incredible amount of authority in the minds of people. Researchers at Duke University's Fuqua School of Business and Canada's University of Waterloo discovered that even fleeting exposure to an established brand can cause us to adopt the behaviors promoted or depicted by those brands.[2]

With all the information that bombards us daily, clear branding helps us make sense of it all. A brand creates a mental shortcut that makes it easier to categorize and remember companies, products, causes, candidates, etc. We have neither the time nor the mental capacity to assess everyone and everything properly. To make sense out of the world, we must fill in the information gaps somehow, so we rely on branding. Therefore, it is critical that we properly brand ourselves and the things we represent, helping people to place them in their proper context.

What was Jesus' brand? In other words, what are the first few things that come to mind when you think about Jesus? Good person? Teacher? Activist? Martyr? Savior? King? Paul writes that Jesus "made of himself no reputation" (Philippians 2:7, KJV). Paul's point here is not that Jesus did not try to instill a particular image of himself in the minds of people. He certainly did want people to think of him in specific ways. Here are a few examples of the descriptive terms Jesus used to brand himself: "bread of life" (John 6:48), "the way, the truth, and the life" (John 14:6), "the good shepherd" (John 10:11), and "the true vine" (John 15:1). If Jesus had not taken control of his brand, we might not even know his name. (I realize this is a strange theological thought experiment.)

The point that Jesus "made of himself no reputation" refers to his *motive* for establishing his personal brand. His motive was not to promote himself; it was to promote his higher purpose. He branded himself as an "access point" for people to experience a relationship with their Creator. He couldn't promote this higher purpose without promoting his own personal brand.

Likewise, nobody can properly understand what you represent without understanding you. Branding yourself intentionally is essential for fulfilling your higher purpose.

Whether we realize it or not, we all have a brand. Companies, charities, churches, cultures, political parties, schools, and even countries each have a brand. Likewise, all individuals have brands: performers, educators, politicians, religious figures, etc. Even your family has a brand. Through the way we conduct ourselves and our organizations, we either establish these brands intentionally, or we allow others to establish our brand solely through their own biases, stereotypes, and prejudices. If a person feels he or she has been largely misunderstood by society, this is often because the person has not taken responsibility for establishing a personal brand. Or the person is delusional about what he or she has been broadcasting into the world.

The world trains us to live with an attitude of false humility. We know we were created to promote something specific and meaningful with our lives, but we have been misled into thinking we can do this without a clearly defined brand.

To some degree, most of us have been muzzled by the fear of looking like a self-promoter, so it becomes easy to rest in a false humility that does not promote anything at all. Yet most of us will find no rest in sitting idly on the sidelines of life, watching everyone else's ideas become realities.

As I work with authors, I find that many people are afraid to have a clear and specific brand, fearing that such focus will "limit", "pigeon-hole", or "type-cast" themselves. They want to have the "flexibility" to become known for many different things. This is pride and fear all at once. The master said in Jesus' Parable of the Minas, "To those who use well what they are given, even more will be given" (Luke 19:26, NLT). The way of Jesus is to be effective and productive with one thing. Good stewardship with that one thing—in this case, your brand—will open the door to success in other areas.

In one sentence, how do you want people to view you? Your organization?

What parts of yourself or your organization are not accurately reflecting your brand?

Does your brand promote a cause greater than yourself and your organization?

---

[1] Martin Lindstrom, *Buyology: Truth and Lies about Why We Buy* (New York: Broadway Books, 2010), Chapter 6.

[2] Martin Lindstrom, *Brandwashed: Tricks Companies Use to Manipulate Our Minds and Persuade Us to Buy* (New York: Crown Business, 2011), 163.

CONNECT: STRATEGY 13

USE STORIES

Members of the nonprofit organization Invisible Children filmed a documentary in 2003 to expose the atrocities of a rebel group in Central Africa known as the Lord's Resistance Army. The film showed how the LRA had been abducting and abusing children, forcing them to become soldiers in its army. The film awakened many people to the plight of these children in Central Africa, but it was not until almost a decade later when awareness about the problem skyrocketed.

In March 2012, Invisible Children released an internet campaign known as "Kony 2012," which called for the arrest of one man who recruited many of these children. Remarkably, the video that was released as part of the campaign was viewed 40 million times in only three days! Rather than presenting mere facts and statistics about the issue, this campaign told a story and put the spotlight on one main antagonist: Joseph Kony.

The founder of Invisible Children also featured his own son in the film to help viewers consider their responses to the issue as if their own child had been forced into Joseph Kony's army.

To deliver his message to people on an emotional level, Jesus told stories about ordinary people and everyday situations. The Greek word for these types of stories is "parabola," which means "comparison, illustration, analogy." Leonard Sweet writes,

> Jesus told between 31 and 65 parables (depending on who's counting). Scholars can't agree whether some are parables or not. But most will admit that at least one-third of Jesus' teachings are parables. They were His brand signature.[1]

Jesus did not illustrate his points through parables to mince words. Quite the opposite! He used these parables, simple stories, to help people *feel* a certain way about his message, which is the most effective form of education. People always had an emotional response to Jesus' parables. Through his stories, his audiences felt the joy of good news, the pain of sadness, and the sting of rebuke. They felt; then, they understood.

Not only did Jesus communicate through stories, but his core message itself was a story. To explain how intensely humans are loved by our Creator despite our self-inflicted flaws, Jesus told three sequential stories that depicted this type of love (see Luke 15). The first story was about a shepherd who had left his 99 sheep to go out and find the one sheep that was lost. Second, he told of a woman who had lost a treasured coin, so she swept the entire house until she found it. As the crescendo of this medley of parables, he told a story about a father whose son rejected him and squandered his inheritance. When the son came back to ask for forgiveness, the father ran to him, restored him to his place in the family, and threw a massive party for him. Leonard Sweet notes,

> Jesus was a Jewish preacher, not a Greek preacher. He majored in images and stories, not in ideas, syllogisms, and propositions. But Jesus chose to communicate biculturally: He had to speak to Greco-Roman linear thinkers and to Hebrew nonlinear thinkers ... Greek is the language of words while Hebrew is the language of images.[2]

Logic affects thinking. Emotions affect behavior. It is not enough to share facts and features about what you are offering. People must be able to feel the joy of someone who possesses what you are offering. Likewise, they must feel the sense of loss by not having it.

Tell a story that illustrates the benefit of what you are offering. Stories connect on an emotional level in a way that helps people to view themselves personally experiencing what you are offering. Until your message is communicated as a story, it's just abstract theory.

What is the plot of the story that your brand is telling?

Who are the main characters in the story that your brand is telling?

If somebody made a movie about the story that your brand is telling, would you pay to see it?

---

[1] Leonard Sweet and Frank Voila, *Jesus: A Theography* (Nashville: Thomas Nelson, 2012), 192.

[2] Ibid., 189.

ASK QUESTIONS

Psychologist and television personality Dr. Phil McGraw has achieved great success with his intervention techniques, which help people to break bad and, often, nasty habits and thought patterns. As the guests on his show attempt to justify their destructive behavior, Dr. Phil famously asks, "How's that working for you?" Why is this question so powerful? It helps people to think critically about their situations. The question invites them to participate in their own intervention.

Jesus was a master of asking tough questions. Why? He wanted a two-way connection with people. He did not just want to preach at them. He wanted a relationship, and relationships require two-way conversations. Further, questions are the best tools to keep conversations going. One scholar noted that 153 of Jesus' questions have been preserved. Tom Hughes observed, "Jesus does not have Q and A sessions. He has Q and Q sessions." Even when Jesus' opponents tried to corner him with a question, he would often respond with a question. Here are a few examples of questions that Jesus asked:

"Who do people say I am?"
"What are you doing more than others?"

"What good will it be for a man if he gains the
  whole world, yet forfeits his soul?"
"Why are you thinking these things?"
"What do you think?"
"What is written in the Law?"

Especially in the Information Age, people want to participate in conversations—not merely lectures. People are not tired of hearing from you; they are tired of hearing from you *about* you. Social media posts that ask a question almost always generate more interest than any other type of post. People want and need to be heard.

Invite your customers, constituents, and prospects into a conversation with you by questioning them about topics that are relevant to your brand. Help them to buy into your message by inviting their feedback.

If your pitch could only consist of questions to close the deal, what would those questions be?

SPEAK IN FRONT OF GROUPS

M any of us have been avoiding public speaking like it's a virus. Are you one of them? If you are intimidated by public speaking, I can relate. My first assignment for my public speaking class in college was simply to "tell a story (any story) for five minutes." At this stage of my life, I had never delivered a formal speech in front of people. About one minute into my talk, I froze. It felt like an out-of-body experience. As the entire class was staring at me awkwardly, I was completely humiliated.

During the next semester, I began Air Force ROTC, a program for training Air Force officers prior to commissioning for active duty. At that point, I had to start giving speeches and briefings nearly every week! Out of necessity, I became much more confident and effective as a public speaker. Soon, I even started getting paid to speak to groups in churches and in other public places.

Public speaking was a massive part of Jesus' marketing strategy. Jesus had a few guys like Matthew and John writing down the things he said, but his focus was on public speaking: one to one, one to a few, and one to many. The *Gospel of Mark* records that "crowds gathered around Him again, and, *according to His custom*, He once more began to teach them." (Mark 10:1, emphasis mine). Public speaking was a "custom" of Jesus Christ, and it should be the custom of anyone seeking to be a great marketer.

Anywhere people gathered, Jesus shared his message with them. He spoke to groups large and small. He spoke in the marketplace, synagogues, in the fields, and at people's homes. Leonard Sweet writes,

> One of Jesus' favorite places to preach was on the Sea of Galilee. Jesus pioneered voice amplification for large crowds by using a boat as His podium, the water as a sounding board, and the sloping hills and curving coves where people would sit as a natural ampitheater.[1]

When he preached at a house in Capernaum, the Bible says "so many gathered that there was no room left" (Mark 2:1-5). Yes, Jesus was a great speaker. But he also spoke frequently. He spoke wherever and whenever people would listen.

Few marketing strategies will help to position you as a trusted expert like speaking in front of a group. Researcher Albert Mehrabian became noteworthy for what he called the "7%-38%-55% Rule." He is the reason why you have probably heard it said that 90 percent of communication is non-verbal. He concluded that only 7 percent of communication is the actual words spoken, 38 percent is the tone of voice, and the other 55 percent of communication is body language. Therefore, a massive percentage of your message simply cannot be communicated through written forms of communication such as books, blogging, social media updates, and direct mail. You must speak to people, audibly and visually, to get your message across as a marketer.

We won't be able to market the way Jesus did unless we become willing to overcome the fear of public speaking and gain experience speaking in front of people regularly. If you are physically able, and you want to market like Jesus, share your message in front of people. Confronting the common fear of public speaking will prove to yourself and to others how much you believe in what you are offering.

When I was in the Air Force, I joined my local Toastmasters group, which gave me the opportunity to practice my public speaking in a supportive environment. You could start recording videos of yourself sharing your message, posting them on YouTube, and then sharing them on social media.

Online webinars are a great way to share your message and get public speaking experience at the same time. Tools like Zoom—which offers a webinar management add-on feature—will allow you to facilitate live seminars and workshops, reaching people anywhere in the world all at once. All you need is a presentation, a webcam, a decent microphone, a computer, and an internet connection.

To attract great new authors to my publishing company, I offered a free, 30-minute live webinar during which I taught the basics of "How to Write, Fund, Publish, and Sell Your Book." Thirty people showed up to the first webinar, and the event resulted in thousands of dollars in revenue for my company.

Whatever you do, if you are physically able and have a message you believe in, get in front of people and speak!

You can do this in-person or online. Do not wait for someone to invite you to speak at their event or conference. If nobody is inviting you to speak at their event, start your own event! There are no excuses!

If you were going to speak to your target group live for 30 minutes tomorrow, what would you talk about?

On what day will you present your next public speaking presentation in-person or via webinar? Be sure to put it on the calendar and start promoting it.

---

[1] Leonard Sweet and Frank Voila, *Jesus: A Theography* (Nashville: Thomas Nelson, 2012), 177-78.

FUNCTION 4

LEAD

"Follow Me, and I will make you become fishers of men."
Mark 1:17

PICK YOUR CORE TEAM FROM YOUR TARGET GROUP

Since seeing the movie *Moneyball*, I have never been able to look at professional sports the same way. The film highlights the disadvantages faced by under-funded Major League Baseball teams as compared to teams with the largest budgets for acquiring the best players. Teams such as the New York Yankees and the Boston Red Sox can afford to hire multiple superstar players while the teams with low funding struggle to win games without multiple superstars.

Based on Michael Lewis' 2003 book by the same title, *Moneyball* depicts how the struggling Oakland Athletics Major League Baseball team used a sophisticated analysis of statistics to recruit the right players during the 2002 season, hoping to compensate for its lack of funding. This use of "sabermetrics" enabled the team to find the right players and win 20 consecutive games, despite their lack of super-star players. Rather than focusing on getting the *best* players, this method of recruiting helped them to get the *right* players. At first, the 2002 Oakland Athletics looked like a rag-tag group that couldn't win games. Soon, they began to gel and achieve success as their strengths complemented each other's.

Jesus' approach to acquiring his closest students and advocates, his inner circle, was quite different from other first-century teachers. Tim Keller writes, "Pupils chose rabbis; rabbis did not choose pupils."[1] Rabbis during this time waited for prospective protégés to approach them and request to study under them, thereby taking on the rabbi's "yoke" of instruction. These young men would have been fervently preparing themselves to follow and ultimately become a rabbi, one of the most distinguished positions in first-century Israel. Rabbis were bastions of the Jewish culture: faith, customs, commerce, education, government, and more. The goal of a rabbi was not merely to preach sermons or to teach workshops. The goal was to make disciples, people who would literally follow and become like the rabbi in every aspect of life.

Going against the tradition of his culture, Jesus went to the fringes of his society to select 12 ordinary men who weren't even pursuing the opportunity to follow or become a rabbi. These unqualified men would constitute his core marketing team. They would become his tribe, his brand ambassadors. While it seems surprising that Jesus would select a group of Jewish outcasts to be his closest advocates, it seems logical considering they were a cross-section of the target group he aimed to reach. He used the ordinary and the outcasts to spread his message among the ordinary and the outcasts. Ultimately, they would take his message to the entire world.

Jesus told his disciples, "You did not choose Me but I chose you, and appointed you" (John 15:16a). Unlike other rabbis, Jesus didn't wait for his followers to come to him. Instead, he selected his protégés carefully and pursued them. When Jesus picked his 12 disciples, he was at once selecting his traveling companions, friends, and ambassadors. This required a thoughtful and prayerful selection process. Leonard Sweet writes,

> A disciple was someone who learned a skill or way of life from a teacher. With respect to Jesus, a disciple was a follower—not just of a set of teachings but of an entire way of living.[2]

He wasn't just selecting a group of people to hear him lecture once per week. He was selecting those with whom he would share his life.

Your core team must represent your target group; otherwise, you may need to redefine your target group. You will tend to attract who you *are*—not necessarily who you *want*—and your organization's identity is defined largely by the individual identities of your core team members. These core team members constitute the culture of your organization, which will attract certain types of people while disinteresting and deterring others.

If Jesus had been targeting the upper echelons of his society, I'm confident he would have ensured that his core team reflected such a group.

Don't spend your time marketing to the crowd. Don't sit around waiting for the crowd to come and follow you. Instead, be proactive and assemble a tribe, beginning by selecting and building your core team from among your target group.

What are the core characteristics of your target group that the members of your core team should possess?

---

[1] Timothy Keller, *Jesus the King* (New York: Riverhead, 2011), 19.

[2] Leonard Sweet and Frank Voila, *Jesus: A Theography* (Nashville: Thomas Nelson, 2012), 131.

AT FIRST, ASK FOR A SMALL COMMITMENT

Pandora Internet Radio is one of my favorite online services. I listen to a personalized movie soundtracks or classical music station—which I've curated over several years—nearly every time I sit down to read or work at my computer. The music inspires me and helps me to be much more productive. I got hooked on Pandora when I started using their free, ad-supported service. Eventually, I decided to pay for the upgrade to Pandora One to get the version without the commercials, the premium version that offers non-stop music for an annual fee.

If I would have had to pay for the premium version before trying out the service, I doubt I would have ever subscribed to Pandora in the first place. Although the commitment was small, I still had to expend a small amount of effort to create an account, log-in, and spend a little time learning the system. Pandora leveraged that small commitment and turned me into a paying customer.

For Jesus, giving something for "free" didn't mean nothing was required from the other person. Though, it always meant the other person was getting the best end of the deal. Nevertheless, there was always an exchange.

People were eager to spend time with Jesus, so getting Jesus' attention was desired by many. Initially, Jesus might ask to borrow the person's boat—as he did with Peter. Or he would ask to come have dinner at the person's house—as he did with Zaccheus. Jesus usually exchanged his time for the opportunity to influence the person—even for a moment. Then, he would leverage that influence to gain greater influence in that person's life—always for a mutual benefit.

Social psychologists Jonathan Freedman and Scott Fraser studied how homeowners in a posh neighborhood responded to requests to display a public service announcement sign in their front yard that said, "Drive Carefully." The researchers found that only 17 percent of homeowners agreed to post the six-feet-by-three-feet sign in their front yard. At the same time, 76 percent of those who previously consented to displaying a small, relatively inconspicuous sign agreed to display the big one. The conclusion of the study was that people are more apt to make a big commitment to someone after they have already made a small commitment.[1]

Don't take the all-or-nothing approach. If you bypass asking for small commitments before asking for a big commitment from someone, you're probably sabotaging your marketing efforts. Create and give value to people constantly, asking them to make small commitments along the way. Invite them to sample your product or service. Invite them to opt into your e-mail list. Invite them to download one of your articles for free. Invite them to attend one of your free events. In this way, your prospect will begin to take ownership of your brand as they taste, see, and benefit from what you're offering. Start with a small commitment. Then, make the "big ask."

In what ways are you allowing your prospects to taste and see what you have to offer before asking for the big commitment?

---

[1] Robert B. Cialdini, Noah J. Goldstein, and Steve J. Martin, *Yes! 50 Scientifically Proven Ways to Be Persuasive* (New York: Free Press, 2008), 65.

BE PROUD TO ASK BIG

While strolling on a sidewalk in Paris, a woman approached renowned artist, Pablo Picasso, as he was sketching. She asked him if he would sketch a portrait of her and assured him she would pay him for his work. He finished a masterpiece within a matter of minutes.

"And what do I owe you?" she asked.

"Five thousand francs," he answered.

"But it only took you three minutes."

"No, Madame. It took me all my life," said Picasso.

Though it's hard to ask people to pay a high price or give a big commitment, Jesus never seemed to hesitate when it came to asking audaciously.

A rich young member of the religious ruling class once came to Jesus and asked, "Good Teacher, what shall I do to inherit eternal life?" (Mark 10:17) He wasn't just asking for healing or for a handout. He was asking for the ultimate: to have eternal life. This wealthy and powerful man tried to convince Jesus that he was a "good person," having obeyed all the laws of his society since he was a boy, yet he sensed that he still wasn't good enough to have eternal life.

Jesus said to him, "One thing you lack: go and sell all you possess and give to the poor, and you will have treasure in heaven; and come, follow Me" (Mark 10:21).

The Bible says that this young man "went away grieving," unwilling to do what Jesus asked him to do (Mark 10:22). This young man's pride in his personal achievement hindered him from committing himself to following Jesus.

Most people would have been too afraid and intimidated to ask such a rich and influential person to make such a massive commitment. Nevertheless, Jesus boldly told this "successful" man to sell everything he had and give the money to the poor before he could fully experience what Jesus was offering.

When it came time to "close the deal" and make the "big ask," Jesus didn't dance around the issue. He asked for massive commitments that carried high costs. Afterall, a high-value reward requires a high-level commitment.

Jesus was proud of what he offered because he was convinced it was in the best interest of people, it fulfilled his higher purpose, and it cost him everything. He gave everything for it because he knew how valuable it was. He compared it to a "a treasure hidden in the field, which a man found and hid again; and from joy over it he goes and sells all that he has and buys that field" just to get the treasure (Matthew 13:44). Money was too cheap to buy what Jesus was offering. It cost people everything they had. Jesus even said,

> If you want to be my disciple, you must hate everyone else by comparison—your father and

mother, wife and children, brothers and sisters—yes, even your own life. Otherwise, you cannot be my disciple. (Luke 14:26, NLT)

Frequently, marketers try to hide the cost of what they are offering, fearing that the cost might scare people away. Jesus did exactly the opposite. Jesus asked for big commitments so audaciously that, at first, it almost seems like he was trying to discourage people from accepting his message and becoming his follower. Of course, it's not that he was trying to discourage people from following him. Rather, he wanted them to count the cost of what he was offering. To illustrate this point, Jesus said,

> For which one of you, when he wants to build a tower, does not first sit down and calculate the cost to see if he has enough to complete it? Otherwise, when he has laid a foundation and is not able to finish, all who observe it begin to ridicule him, saying, "This man began to build and was not able to finish." Or what king, when he sets out to meet another king in battle, will not first sit down and consider whether he is strong enough with ten thousand *men* to encounter the one coming against him with twenty thousand? Or else, while the other is still far away, he sends a delegation and asks for terms of peace. So then, none of you can be My disciple who does not give up all his own possessions. (Luke 14:28-33)

How difficult is it for you to ask people to commit to what you're offering? Yes, there's a season for asking for small commitments. At some point, though, it's time to make the "big ask." It's usually easy for us to describe our products, services, and causes. It's much more uncomfortable to ask somebody directly to take a specific action:

> "Buy my product."
> "Subscribe to my service."
> "Sign up for this cause."
> "Donate to this charity."
> "Vote for me."
> "Join my team."

There are few things more frustrating than trying to market something we don't truly believe in. When the time comes to make the "big ask" from a client, constituent, or prospect, you must be convinced firmly of *why* you are marketing. Simon Sinek said, "People don't buy what you do. They buy why you do it." People are loyal to organizations whose messages are more significant than their products and services. Without the right inward motives, you can never be truly proud of what you're offering, which will cause you to undervalue it. When you are confident in what you're offering and why you are offering it, you'll find it much easier to ask people to commit to it at the right cost.

Do you truly believe in what you are offering? Are you convinced of the value that you are delivering to people? A carpenter once fixed a squeaky floor and left a $50 invoice that said, "Hammering = $2, Knowing where to hammer = $48)." Yes, it is critical to allow people to "taste and see" what you're offering before asking them for a big commitment. After they have "tasted and seen," ask for a commitment that matches the value you're offering.

In what areas do you need to ask for a greater level of commitment from the members of your core group? Is it time to raise your standards? Is it time to raise your prices?

INSPIRE YOUR TRIBE TO OWN YOUR VISION

As many college students will tell you, Wikipedia's collaboratively edited, multilingual, and free online encyclopedia is one of the most amazing things ever made. As of the time of this writing, Wikipedia is comprised of 30 million articles in 287 languages and has an estimated 365 million readers.

Jimmy Wales, co-founder of Wikipedia, has led this effort to provide free knowledge to the world almost entirely through a labor force of volunteers. From the beginning, Wales has empowered these volunteer writers, researchers, and editors through inspiring them with his vision to change the world through free knowledge. Anyone can create and edit the articles. Yet, Jimmy Wales didn't help Wikipedia achieve such an astronomical level of success by operating as a dictator within the Wikipedia community. Instead, he empowers the members of the community with a sense of ownership of his vision to provide free knowledge to the world. Because Wikipedia is one of the top-ranked websites in the major search engines, every article the community creates broadens the reach and impact of Wikipedia.

Jesus constantly reinforced his vision in the hearts and minds of his marketing team, which helped them to remain committed. They made Jesus' vision their own. As they shared their lives together, everything Jesus taught his disciples through his words and actions was an expression of their shared vision. He took responsibility for helping them to stay focused on what they were trying to accomplish together.

When Peter was ready to be restored after betraying and denying Jesus, Jesus immediately reminded him of their shared vision to spread the gospel message by serving people. Jesus asked him three times, "Do you love me?" (John 21:15-17)

Peter replied three times, "Yes, I love you."

Jesus responded, "Then, feed my sheep." Despite Peter's failure, Jesus empowered him and called forth his destiny to be a world-changer.

Before he was crucified, Jesus affirmed his disciples with these words: "You are those who have stood by me in my trials" (Luke 22:28). They stood with him, in part, because they owned his vision. Yes, they wrestled with doubt, fear, and self-preservation. Yet, Jesus' followers were committed wholeheartedly to helping him deliver his message to the world. Yes, it was Jesus' vision. At the same time, his followers made it their own because Jesus inspired them. John Ortberg writes,

> Jesus inspired a wealthy cheat named Zacchaeus to give away most of his fortune. He inspired a Samaritan woman to become an evangelist, and she inspired so many townspeople that they had Jesus—a Jewish rabbi—stay in their Samaritan

town and teach them for two solid days. He inspired Peter to get out of his boat. He inspired a woman named Joanna, whose husband, Cusa, worked for a man named Herod who killed John the Baptist and kept trying to kill Jesus. Joanna used money they made working for Herod to help finance Jesus' ministry. He inspired four friends of a paralytic to punch a hole through a roof to get their friend to him. He inspired a woman who had been bleeding for twelve years to fight through a crowd just to touch the hem of his robe.[1]

For Jesus, marketing was a collaborative process that required a team effort and a shared vision. He compared marketing to fishing, saying, "Follow me and I will make you fishers of men" (Mark 1:17). These were commercial fishermen—not amateurs. They didn't use a rod and reel to catch fish by themselves. Instead, they worked together to catch massive amounts of fish with large nets. It wasn't something that could be done effectively by individuals. He needed each one of them to buy in and take ownership of his vision.

Do the people you're marketing to feel a sense of ownership for your vision, or are they just consumers? Would they carry forth your vision even if you weren't around anymore?

---

[1] John Ortberg, *Who Is This Man: The Unpreditable Impact of the Inescapable Jesus* (Grand Rapids: Zondervan, 2012), 62.

LIVE YOUR MESSAGE

At least 2.2 billion people have gathered to listen to Rev. Billy Graham speak throughout his lifetime. At the beginning of his ministry in 1948, he gathered his small team in Modesto, California to establish the guidelines that would help to enable the impact and legacy of the Billy Graham Evangelistic Association. This pact became known as the "Modesto Manifesto." It was an agreement among the leaders in the organization to embody the values they preached:

1. Live free of the love of money by establishing modest salaries for each member.
2. Strictly avoid all perceptions of impropriety.
3. Abstain from making any extravagant claims about the success of the organization.
4. Abstain from criticizing others and their respective organizations.

Rev. Graham was not content to spread a message that he and the members of his organization did not personally embody. As a result of these high standards of personal character, at least 3.2 million people have accepted the message he proclaimed at his evangelistic crusades around the world, and his influence has made an impact at all levels of society. Professor of Christian History at Duke University, Grant Wacker, has said,

> By the middle 1960s, he had become the "Great Legitimator." ... His presence conferred sanctity on events, authority on presidents, acceptability on wars, desirability on decency, [and] shame on indecency ... By the middle 1970s, many deemed him "America's pastor."

Jesus always practiced what he preached. Although he was constantly pressured to violate his message, his methods always reflected his message.

During the first century, the Roman governor in Jerusalem established a tradition of releasing a prisoner each year. Before Jesus was taken away to be crucified, the crowd was given the opportunity to get Jesus released from prison and spared from execution. Instead of voting to release Jesus, they voted to release the convicted murderer, Barabbas. The Bible says the crowd cried out, "Not this man, but Barabbas" (John 18:40). There is little doubt that the vote was rigged, yet there was still a significant amount of people who actually wanted Barabbas to be released instead of Jesus. They wanted to spare a murderer rather than Jesus? How could this be?

Barabbas wasn't just known as a murderer. He was known as a Jewish freedom fighter, a political activist and insurrectionist. The Jewish people were weary and frustrated with being occupied and controlled by the Romans. Barabbas had proven that he was willing to revolt violently against the Roman occupiers. Above all, the Jewish people wanted sovereignty as a nation once again. While the masses hoped that Jesus would lead the revolt against the Romans, most of them had given up that hope as they learned more about his message about an "unseen Kingdom." They didn't yet realize that Jesus was not like other kings. Jesus told his captor, "My kingdom is not of this world" (John 18:36a).

Though Jesus could have easily accomplished a physical overthrow of the government, he stayed true to his vision and his message. People tried to convince him that he could establish his kingdom by means of force, leveraging the strength of the masses who were following him. When the temple guards came to seize him by force, Jesus said, "Am I leading a rebellion ... that you have come out with swords and clubs to capture me?" (Mark 14:43) Most of them still couldn't understand that Jesus wasn't interested in leading a physical overthrow of the government. Even Peter, one of his closest disciples, drew a sword and tried to defend Jesus by force. Jesus rebuked him, saying, "Put your sword back into its place; for all those who take up the sword shall perish by the sword" (Matthew 26:52).

Although Jesus never led an army nor held a public office, the movement he led resulted in the end of emperor worship. His movement inspired such governmental documents as the Magna Carta and the U.S. Constitution, which declared that "all men are created equal; that they are endowed by their Creator with certain unalienable rights."

The more you embody your message, staying true to your principles, the more effective you will become. You wouldn't buy a product or service from someone who wouldn't buy their own stuff, so refuse to allow a disconnection between your message and your methods. Don't sell out your character. Don't compromise your vision. Don't allow social, political, or economic pressures to cause you to redirect your attention away from your core message, vision, and identity. Always embody your message, practicing what you preach. Lead by example and stay on message. As Albert Schweitzer said, "Example isn't the main thing in influencing others. It is the only thing."

What are the things that tempt you to compromise your core message and vision?

PRESENT YOUR MESSAGE CONSISTENTLY

Most gym owners will tell you that January is their busiest month of the year. People start off each New Year with visions of becoming fit, healthy, and toned. In hopes of achieving their goals, they purchase a one-year gym membership. By February, gym attendance is back down to pre-January levels, primarily consisting of the people who already have been physically active for most of their lives (e.g., former high school athletes, etc.). Everyone else wasted their money on a gym membership they don't use. It's no coincidence that they don't renew their memberships the following year, causing their gyms to lose 70 percent of their members at the end of each year. Why?

After the initial sale of the gym membership, most of the gyms don't consistently remind their members of why they joined in the first place. Afterall, they already paid their money ... right? As Jay Levinson said, "68 percent of all business lost is lost owing to apathy after the sale."[1] Yet it costs approximately one-sixth as much to sell something to a current customer than to a prospective customer.[2] Like most gyms, the marketing focus usually is placed almost exclusively on acquiring new members—not on retaining current members. For this reason, many organizations are like a revolving door of commitment; members, customers, clients, donors, and constituents are leaving almost as fast as they entered. In many organizations and industries, people are leaving even faster than they are entering.

When Jesus' followers first began following him, he didn't view their initial commitment as a done deal. He realized his work with them had only begun as they were prone to abandoning him permanently at any point. He knew it was his daily responsibility to invite them to follow him and constantly showing them why they should. Because of his commitment to them, he became frustrated and disappointed with them, at times, for rejecting him and his message.

One of his closest followers, Peter, rejected Jesus to the point of denying that he even knew him—three times! Even after three years of hearing Jesus' message and seeing him demonstrate it, Peter still wasn't fully committed. Yet Jesus didn't give up on him. Before Jesus ascended to Heaven, Peter was the one he put in charge, the "rock" upon which he chose to build his church (Matthew 16:18). Jesus restored him, commissioning him to "shepherd [his] sheep" (John 21:16). Although Peter's betrayal seemed to indicate that he had fallen away completely, Jesus saw it as an opportunity to reinforce his message.

Focus on being a good steward of the influence you currently have by keeping your tribe focused on why they joined with you in the first place. Many experts have observed that people must hear a marketer's message at least seven times before they will accept it. Because Jesus viewed marketing as a process, he understood that people would not make increasingly higher levels of commitment unless they heard his message continually. He wasn't just trying to achieve some flash-in-the-pan, short-lived success through one-time commitments. He wanted to make an impact on generations of people through life-long relationships. He cared too much for people to allow them to slide back into a mediocre life after making only a one-time commitment to his vision.

Jesus knew that when a few key people became transformed by his message over the course of time, they would share it with as many people as possible, for as long as it took, and no matter what the cost. Their testimonies would be credible because they would demonstrate his message with their lives, having been constantly taught and developed by Jesus. Not only were Jesus' disciples his evangelists, they were the living examples of what he was offering to the world.

Advertising isn't fundamentally about billboards and TV commercials. It's about helping people to encounter your message consistently, resulting in familiarity that spreads. It's not a one-time activity. Al Ries said, "Advertising is not a sledge hammer. It's more like a light fog, a very light fog that envelops your prospects."[3] Influence happens in perpetuity—not all at once. Don't confuse communicating your message with asking for something. Yes, there will be a time to ask for greater commitments but spend most of your time displaying the value you are creating for people.

As you put your message in front of people consistently, you may feel like you're being intrusive. That's not necessarily the case. One of my previous mentors used to tell me, "If they love you, they'll want to hear from you con-sistently." Constantly remind your core group about why they decided to buy into your message in the first place.

What percentage of your marketing program is focused on re-cruiting new people into your tribe, and what percentage is fo-cused on developing your current tribe into your marketing team?

---

[1] Levinson, Jay Conrad. *Guerrilla Marketing* (Boston: Houghton Mifflin, 2007), 6.

[2] Ibid., 81.

[3] Al Ries and Jack Trout, *Positioning: The Battle for Your Mind* (New York: McGraw-Hill, 2001), 6.

MULTIPLY

"You shall be My witnesses both in Jerusalem,
and in all Judea and Samaria, and
even to the remotest part of the earth."
Jesus (from Acts 1:8)

LEVERAGE THE SPIRITUAL POWER OF IDEAS

The film *Inception* by Christopher Nolan tells of a world in which people have the ability to mentally break into each other's subconscious thoughts to extract information and implant thoughts. In the film, the process of invading another person's subconscious is referred to as "inception." Although we may want to assume that our minds are impenetrable, except for the information we consciously choose to allow in, the human mind is actually quite vulnerable and impressionable. Thoughts are more powerful than most people realize.

Everything we see began as a thought. Marketers manifest and propagate these creative, unseen thoughts through a variety of means. Thoughts, if they become materialized through action, can spread like wildfire. Victor Hugo said, "Nothing, not all the armies of the world, can stop an idea whose time has come." Marketers, strategic influencers, are those that leverage this power with a specific goal.

Jesus grew up in a society that educated its people on the spiritual power of ideas. In the Jewish worldview, everything began as an idea, a thought that materialized into the physical world. The Bible says, "What is seen was not made out of things which are visible" (Hebrews 11:3). Jesus understood that marketing an idea to influence people was a spiritual endeavor, not merely a commercial or intellectual one.

In the "Parable of the Sower" (Mark 4:3-25), Jesus described his message as a "seed" that was available to everyone. He compared different types of people to different types of soil. Some people would not receive the "seed" of his message because they were like hard and rocky soil, unable to allow the seed to take root and grow. Everybody had the opportunity to receive what Jesus was offering, but many weren't prepared to receive it.

Marketing is a spiritual endeavor. The challenge of marketing is to get thoughts to penetrate a person's conscious and subconscious thinking. Jay Levinson writes, "Marketing is the art of getting people to change their minds—or to maintain their mindsets if they're already inclined to do business with you."[1] Marketers get ideas into their own minds and then begin to implant those ideas systematically into the minds of other people. As a marketer, you aren't merely offering products and services; you are implanting ideas spiritually, in seed form, into the minds of people.

Having received this ability from our Creator, we are all stewards of this power as we are all using it to some degree—whether we realize it or not. As we become more highly skilled at marketing, the level of stewardship and accountability increases.

Do you approach marketing as a spiritual endeavor? Why or why not?

[1] Jay Conrad Levinson, *Guerrilla Marketing* (Boston: Houghton Mifflin, 2007), 3.

GET CONVERSATIONS GOING

As a self-published Christian novel with very little spent on marketing, William P. Young's *The Shack* became the #1 trade fiction book on the *New York Times Best Seller* list from June 2008 to early 2010. Unable to get a traditional publishing deal in the early days, Young and his team of two publicists, Brad Cummings and Wayne Jacobsen, had to market the book solely from the grassroots level. They sold the book out of a garage and promoted the book directly through churches, Christian-themed blogs, and a series of podcasts described as "an ever-expanding conversation among those thinking outside the box of organized religion." As they spread the book's controversial ideas and themes that are intensely familiar to the human experience, the trio started a massive conversation about the book's subject matter that resulted in more than 10 million copies sold.

Everywhere Jesus went, he stimulated conversations about his message, and those conversations spread like wildfire. His longest conversation on record happened with a Samaritan woman at a well (John 4:7-30). Jesus asked the woman for a drink of water, and she was shocked! The

Samaritan woman said to Him, "How is it that You, being a Jew, ask me for a drink of water since I am a Samaritan woman?" (John 4:9) This woman was the epitome of the type of person any respectable Jewish man would never chat with—especially in public. First, she was a Samaritan, which the Jews considered inferior and half-breeds. Paul Johnson explains,

> The Samaritans were hated by the Jews ... [with] a quasi-religious fury and a form of local racism of the most ferocious temper.[1]

On top of that, she was a woman, and no well-regarded Jewish man would have been caught talking to a woman in a public place. Furthermore, she was divorced and was living in immorality with a man who was not her husband. Considering she was drawing her own water, we can also infer that this woman was poor.

As they stood at the well, Jesus used the water as a metaphor to explain his message of eternal hope, helped her to become convicted about her sin of adultery, and taught her about worshipping God. This encounter made such a profound impact on the woman that she immediately went back to her town to spread the word about the remarkable man she just met at the well. The Bible says,

> So the woman left her waterpot, and went into the city and said to the men, "Come, see a man who told me all the things that I have done." (John 4:28-29)

As a result of their conversation,

... from that city many of the Samaritans believed in Him because of the word of the woman
who testified, "He told me all the things I have
done." So when the Samaritans came to Jesus,
they were asking Him to stay with them; and He
stayed there two days. Many more believed because of His word. (John 4:39-41)

Because of an unforgettable one-on-one conversation
with Jesus, the woman at the well went back and testified
about it among her own people. The people became so cu-
rious that they had to see for themselves.

In his book, *Word of Mouth Marketing*, Andy Sernovitz
says, "Advertising is the price of being boring." It is some-
what easy and expensive to rely on passive forms of marketing to get our messages across, such as fancy graphics,
e-mail blasts, direct mail, TV spots, and other media. Yet it
has been proven over and over that word-of-mouth conversations are the most effective form of advertising—by a
longshot. Jonah Berger, author of *Contagious*, said that
"every day, the average American engages in more than
sixteen word-of-mouth episodes, separate conversations
where they say something positive or negative about an organization, brand, product, or service."[2] Get your message
injected into these conversations.

The word of mouth doesn't necessarily have to be positive to increase the spread of your message. Jonah Berger
writes, "For books by new or relatively unknown authors,
negative reviews increased sales by 45 percent."[3] As Oscar
Wilde wrote in *The Picture of Dorian Gray*, when it comes to
word-of-mouth, "There is only one thing in the world

worse than being talked about, and that is not being talked about."

I saw hundreds of food carts when I lived in New York City. Usually, the cart attendant was just standing there without any customers, keeping their pretzels or meats-on-sticks hot until a customer stopped by. One major exception is Halal Chicken and Gyro on 53rd and 6th Avenue.

When I first noticed this particular cart late one night, there was a line halfway down the block. While there are several food carts within a few blocks that are nearly identical, serving the same food almost the same way, there is rarely a wait to get their food. At Halal Chicken and Gyro on 53rd and 6th, people gladly wait in line for as long as an hour.

This famous food cart originally began as a hot dog cart back in 1990, a time when nearly every food cart in New York City was selling hot dogs. The Egyptian man who owned the cart decided to do something different—something remarkable. Instead of selling hot dogs, he began to sell tasty platters of chicken and lamb, seasoned rice, and pita bread. This new approach to the street food business got conversations going.

Initially, the conversation was about how unique and delicious the food was. Then, at some point, people began to discuss the "long lines at Halal Chicken and Gyro." Although there are now many food carts in New York City that have attempted to copy the food cart at 53rd Street and 6th Avenue, nobody is talking about the "long lines" at those other food carts. Their lines aren't long because they haven't done anything remarkable. They merely attempted to duplicate exactly what someone else did. As a result, nobody is remarking about them.

Word-of-mouth marketing is about giving people one good reason to talk about what you're offering and then making it easier for that conversation to happen. If you want to be remarkable, give people something to remark about.

What creative things can you do to get more people talking about your message and your brand?

---

[1] Paul Johnson, *Jesus: A Biography from a Believer* (New York: Viking, 2010), 50.

[2] Jonah Berger, *Contagious: Why Things Catch On* (New York: Simon & Schuster, 2013), 64.

[3] Ibid., 81.

MULTIPLY: STRATEGY 24

ENCOURAGE YOUR TRIBE TO SHARE TESTIMONIES

In its heyday, Hotmail grew to 18 million users and was sold for $400 million. Its success was due almost entirely to including this statement with a link at the bottom of each e-mail sent by its users: "Get your free e-mail with Hotmail." Every e-mail from an @hotmail.com account was transformed into a word-of-mouth marketing seed that created more awareness and credibility for the Hotmail brand. Every e-mail became a testimony from the sender that said implicitly, "I trust and rely on this service provider. You can, too."

After Jesus served people, he encouraged them to go and testify to others about what he had done for them—*with a few exceptions that will be discussed in the "Bonus Strategy" at the end of this book*. After delivering the man possessed by a demon at Gadara, Jesus told him, "Go home to your people and report to them what great things the Lord has done for you, and how He had mercy on you" (Mark 5:19). The Bible says that "he went away and began to proclaim in Decapolis what great things Jesus had done for him; and everyone was amazed" (Mark 5:20).

At the end of his time of service on earth, Jesus told his disciples, "You shall be My witnesses both in Jerusalem, and in all Judea and Samaria, and even to the remotest part of the earth" (Acts 1:8). He commissioned them to testify to the world of everything they had seen, heard, and experienced with Jesus.

No story is more effective as a marketing tool than the testimony of a person who has benefited from you, your message, your product, your service, or your cause. Aim to get a testimonial endorsement from the people that benefit from what you're offering. Be aggressive about getting feedback on how your product, service, cause, or message is changing lives. Archive this feedback carefully and share your positive reviews and testimonies with others.

Many people don't buy anything on Amazon.com without first scanning the ratings and reviews for the products they are considering. The social proof of a 5-star rating and a positive review is extremely powerful in encouraging someone to buy a particular product.

When I launched the *Theology of Business Podcast*, the main thing I requested from my tribe was that they leave a rating and review for the podcast in the iTunes Store. These early ratings and reviews made a tremendous impact on boosting the *Theology of Business Podcast* in iTunes' rankings. If the ratings and reviews stop, iTunes will punish my podcast in the rankings. That's how it works. (So, please go leave a review for the *Theology of Business Podcast* on your favorite podcast platform!)

Many people won't share testimonies about you unless you ask them to. Some people may feel they need to have your permission to talk about you publicly. Go ahead and deputize them as part of your word-of-mouth marketing team.

Who are the people you need to ask for a written or video testimonial of how you (or your organization) have made their lives better?

INJECT FRESH MOMENTUM

In the movie *Field of Dreams*, Terence Mann (James Earl Jones) assures Ray Kinsella (Kevin Costner) that, if he builds the thing he's been dreaming about, "People will come." However, the real world is not like the field of dreams. People won't support your cause if they don't hear about it. This requires building momentum behind your message, which enables it to spread.

Jesus was constantly moving from town to town. Each time he visited or revisited a city was an opportunity to inject fresh momentum into his marketing. He took advantage of these momentum-building opportunities. When Jesus went to a new town, he would send a team of promoters to campaign in that town in advance of his coming. Even Jesus didn't assume many people would show up to hear him without some advance promotion to get people talking about his coming.

As an example of how Jesus built momentum behind his message, the *Gospel of Luke* tells us, "Now after this the Lord appointed seventy others, and sent them in pairs ahead of Him to every city and place where He Himself was going to come" (Luke 10:1). They were to take nothing with them except for Jesus' message and the clothes on their back—not even shoes. Jesus instructed this marketing team of 35 pairs to invite themselves into people's homes and serve them in the ways Jesus modeled for them. Whenever they came to a house where the host accepted them, they were to remain with the host and share Jesus' message with them. In this way, Jesus built a tremendous amount of anticipation and "buzz" in advance of his arrival.

It would be a shame to work hard developing your product, service, or event and release it without any significant momentum behind it. Before you launch your stuff, make sure people are expecting it. Give them just enough information to get them excited about what is to come. Deputize them as part of your launch team.

Fear is to either do nothing or to try doing it all at once. While you may be anxious to launch your next product or service, make sure you have first built a sufficient amount of momentum to generate word-of-mouth marketing.

For your next product, service, or event launch, create a six-month schedule that includes all the events and other momentum-building activities that you (and/or your organization) are planning in support of the launch.

BONUS STRATEGY

LEVERAGE THE RIGHT TIMING

When I was living in New York City as a single guy, I traveled back to visit some friends in Virginia Beach, which is where I attended graduate school. While I was there, I went to a friend's birthday party one evening. As soon as I walked in, I immediately saw the most beautiful woman I have ever seen in my life, standing down the long hallway in front of me. I thought, "I need to meet her!" Later on at the party that night, we met and had a great conversation.

After I found out from a mutual friend that she was single, I decided to contact her via e-mail when I returned to New York City. We traded a few quick e-mails, and then I asked her if she wanted to talk on the phone. She said, "I'm busy with law school but maybe later…" Well, I can take a hint. Either she didn't like me, or it was just the wrong timing. I chose to believe it was just the timing.

So, four months later, I decided to give it another shot. I sent a quick, one-sentence question to her. She responded with several paragraphs, so I knew I had made it to the next step in the application process toward becoming her husband. I took her on our first date (to the Busch Gardens theme park) two weeks later, and we got married less than one year later.

The "Law of Timing" is one of John Maxwell's *21 Irrefutable Laws of Leadership*. It states, "When to lead is as important as what to do and where to go." Jesus was a master of the law of timing. His followers and family members frequently tried to pressure him into rushing his timetable, but he refused to sacrifice the right timing for what seemed expedient to others.

Though he must have felt some pressure to launch his public ministry in his 20s or sooner, Jesus waited until he was 30 years old to begin his public ministry. In Jesus' culture, 30 was the age for authority, and the Old Testament indicates that the minimum age for a priest was 30 years old (Numbers 4:2-3). Prior to this time, he was being prepared for the three-year period during which he would turn the world upside-down.

After his public ministry began, Jesus remained sensitive about the timing of delivering certain aspects of his message. When Jesus was in Galilee, his brothers said to him,

> Leave here and go into Judea, so that Your disciples also may see Your works which You are doing. No one works in secret who seeks to be known openly. If you do these things, do them in front of the world. (John 7:4)

Although he may have broadened his influence by going to Judea at that time, he refused to allow his brothers to rush his timetable. Jesus responded to them, "My time is not yet here" (John 7:6a). Later, when the time was right, he said, "Let us go to Judea again" (John 11:7a). He wouldn't allow his timing to be dictated by others' rashness and ignorance.

Because he wanted to reveal certain things at certain times, there are several instances recorded in the Gospels in which Jesus performed a miracle for someone and then told them to keep quiet about it. Scholars refer to this motif as the "Messianic Secret," which occurs mainly in the *Gospel of Mark*. After Jesus healed a leper, he said to the man, "See that you say nothing to anyone" (Mark 1:44a). Does that seem absurd? If we were trying to transform the lives of every single person in the world with our message, why would we ever say to a person who was just powerfully impacted by our service offering, "Don't tell anybody about this?" Chances are, we wouldn't. Yet Jesus did. Despite Jesus' instruction, the man

> ... went out and began to proclaim it freely and to spread the news around, to such an extent that Jesus could no longer publicly enter a city, but stayed out in unpopulated areas; and they were coming to Him from everywhere.
> (Mark 1:45)

When Peter first told Jesus that he believed his message, the Bible says "He [Jesus] warned them to tell no one about Him" (Mark 8:30). Why would he tell his core marketing team to not tell people about him?

At times, perhaps Jesus delayed because he needed the first part of his ministry to select, recruit, and develop the few close disciples who would carry on his work after his ministry, death, resurrection, and ascension. This was a critical part of laying the foundation for the Church he was establishing.

In some instances, it seems clear that he didn't do things according to others' timetables because he might have been killed before he had the opportunity to spread his message. As an example, the Bible says, "He was unwilling to walk in Judea because the Jews were seeking to kill Him" (John 7:1). Jesus shook things up everywhere he went, but some areas were more dangerous than others. The wisdom of Jesus led him to wait when others wanted to rush and to move when others wanted to wait.

Scholars have offered several explanations for the "Messianic Secret." The only conclusion we can be certain of is that, when it came to timing, Jesus operated counter-intuitively from how most of us tend to operate. His disciples frequently tried to pressure him into launching his worldwide campaign half-cocked. They couldn't understand why he would delay building his public platform.

If you try to release the right product, service, or message at the wrong time, it will fall flat. Like Jesus, we need to be strategic and thoughtful to ensure we don't violate the law of timing.

Have you thoughtfully considered the timeline for each step in your marketing campaign? "Leverage the Right Timing" doesn't mean necessarily you should delay. It just means you should be strategic and deliberate about when to accomplish the various steps in your overall marketing plan.

OPEN THE SUPPLY LINE

At the end of World War II, the Communists cut off all outside food, heating oil, and other relief supplies from reaching the citizens of West Berlin, Germany. The Communists' hope was that the West Berliners would become so desperate for their basic necessities that they would put their faith in Communism and the government, abandoning their hope in a free market.

The United States decided it would not stand back and allow this to happen. Despite that the Communists were blocking the free world's access to West Berlin, the US launched a relief effort that became known as the "Berlin Airlift." Because the roads were blocked, the US used its military aircraft to deliver millions of pounds of supplies to provide relief and sustenance for the people. This was the first major logistical airlift in history. Soon thereafter, the Communist blockade against its own people was lifted. More than physical relief, the Berlin Airlift provided hope for desperate people.

During my experience as a US Air Force logistics officer, we provided essential and even vital supplies to people in both combat and humanitarian relief situations. Logistics is the process of getting the right people, things, and *ideas* from one place to another. The root of the Greek-originated word, *logistics,* is the word, *logos,* which means, "word." It's about getting tangible (and intangible) things to the right people at the right place at the right time.

Jesus understood that the world—like the West Berliners with their supply lines cut off—is desperate to hear and receive the message that he wanted to spread. The supply line that gave people faith, hope, and love had been severed. Jesus came to repair that supply line.

Like Jesus, we have an opportunity to market more than products and services. We have the privilege of spreading messages that can transform people's lives. In the long run, we'll be much more effective in our marketing endeavors when we're marketing like Jesus. If you want to do marketing like Jesus, the world needs to hear from you.

"Jesus did many other things ..."
John 21:25

ABOUT THE AUTHOR

Darren Shearer is the founder and director of the Theology of Business Institute, a research and education organization equipping marketplace Christians to explore and apply God's will for business. He is the developer the *Biblical Standards for Businesses Course*, which is being used by colleges and universities internationally. He has authored three books, including *The Marketplace Christian: A Practical Guide to Using Your Spiritual Gifts in Business*.

Darren is also the founder and CEO of High Bridge Books & Media, a multimedia publishing company that publishes and promotes the world-changing ideas of inspiring thought leaders.

A former Captain in the United States Air Force, Darren earned the United States Air Force Commendation Medal for his meritorious service in Kuwait during Operation Iraqi Freedom.

He holds a M.A. in Practical Theology from Regent University (Virginia Beach, VA), an Advanced Graduate Certificate in Management from Pace University (New York, NY), and a B.A. in English from Charleston Southern University (Charleston, SC).

Darren and his wife, Marie, reside in the Great Smoky Mountains of Western North Carolina with their three young boys.

To connect with Darren or to contact him about speaking at an upcoming event, you may contact him via the following:

E-mail: **Darren@HighBridgeMedia.com**
Web: **www.TheologyofBusiness.com/contact**
Twitter: **@DarrenShearer**
Facebook: **www.Facebook.com/BusinessTheology**

Made in the USA
Las Vegas, NV
17 November 2022

59683267R00085